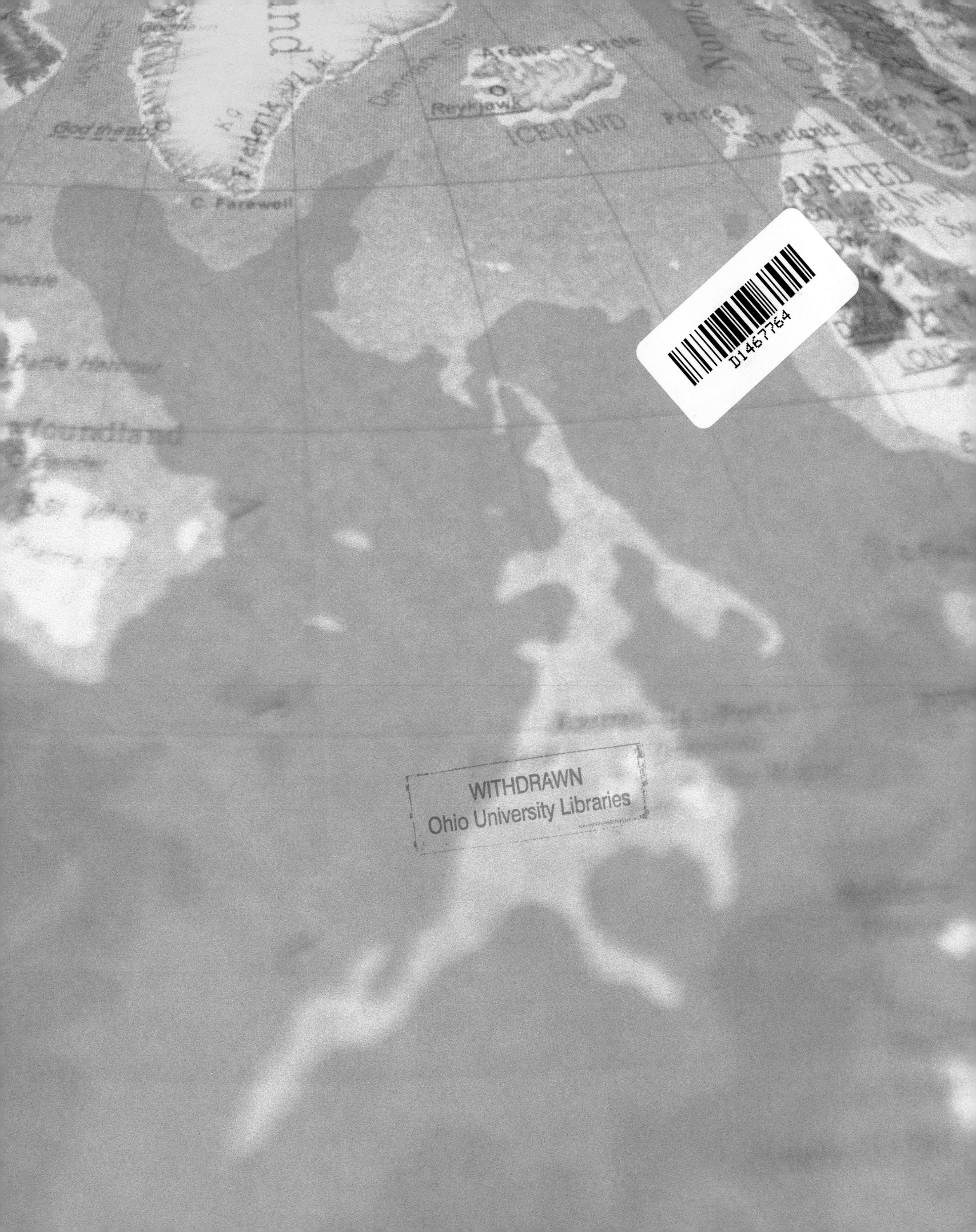
ICELAND
C. Farewell

AN ASSEMBLY OF TASTES

the culinary world of the united nations

a milestone-millennium press publication

JEANNIE LAU

PUBLISHER MILESTONE-MILLENNIUM PRESS

CHIEF EDITOR TAN JU KUANG

DESIGN CONSULTANT IMMORTAL DESIGN SINGAPORE

ILLUSTRATOR YEN ONG

PHOTOGRAPHER DAVID PHAN PHOTOGRAPHY

COLOUR SEPARATOR SINGAPORE SANG CHOY

COLOUR SEPARATION PTE LTD

PRINTED IN CHINA

A CATALOGUE RECORD FOR THIS BOOK IS AVAILABLE FROM

THE NATIONAL LIBRARY OF SINGAPORE

ISBN 981-04-2619-4 FIRST EDITION

ENDORSED BY SINGAPORE NATIONAL

BOOK DEVELOPMENT COUNCIL

ENDORSED BY UNIFEM, NEW YORK, UNITED NATIONS

DEVELOPMENT FUNDS UNIT FOR WOMEN AND CHILDREN

LC Control Number

2001   307030

acknowlegement

A project of this size and stature cannot see fruition without help from all quarters. We would like to thank all the individuals at UN embassies and consulates, as well as their respective tourism boards, all around the world for their kind and comprehensive assistance. The time taken in providing us with information regarding their rich culinary culture, and in supplying us with the recipes, has been integral in producing a publication of this calibre.

As a departure from convention, the production of *An Assembly of Tastes – The Culinary World of the United Nations* was funded by corporate and individual sponsorships. We are extremely grateful to all the individuals and companies who have shared our vision. Thank you for helping us open the eyes of the world to the wonderful cornucopia of food from all the countries in the United Nations.

This book is also, in no small part, the result of the indomitable and enthusiastic collaboration of several individuals whose roles were absolutely instrumental. Many of these companies and individuals have donated their time and expertise in acknowledgement of the charitable nature of this project.

We would like to thank Priscilla Lau, Magdalene Siew, and Chong Kok Lee for their tireless efforts in liaising with the various UN consulates; David Phang Photography for giving life to the pages through their pictures; and Immortal Design whose creativity and imagination permeates the entire essence of the book.

In particular, we would like to thank the following embassies, consulates and tourism boards for their help.

High Commission of the People's Republic of
   Bangladesh, *singapore*
Royal Embassy of Cambodia, *singapore*
Trade and Tourism of Portugal, *bangkok, thailand*
Embassy of the Republic of Argentina, *singapore*
Embassy of Japan, *singapore*
Royal Danish Embassy, *singapore*
Embassy of the Republic of Korea, *singapore*
Embassy of Peru, *singapore*
Embassy of the Lao People's Democratic
   Republic, *singapore*
Royal Embassy of Belgium, *singapore*
Embassy of Mexico, *singapore*
Embassy of Chile, *singapore*
Embassy of the Arab Republic of Egypt, *singapore*
Embassy of the Republic of Italy, *singapore*
Embassy of Ukraine, *jakarta, indonesia*
British High Commission, *singapore*
Embassy of the United States of America,
   singapore
Embassy of the Federal Republic of Germany,
   singapore
French Embassy, *singapore*
Malaysia Tourism Promotion Board, *singapore*
Embassy of the Republic of Guatemala,
   tokyo, japan
Embassy of the Republic of Poland, *singapore*
Embassy of the Kingdom of Morocco, *jakarta,
   indonesia*
High Commission of the Republic of
   South Africa, *singapore*
Embassy of the Federal Democratic Republic
   of Ethiopia, *beijing, china*
Embassy of the Republic of Turkey, *singapore*
Permanent Mission of the Republic of
   Macedonia, *new york, u.s.a.*
High Commission of India, *singapore*
High Commission of Jamaica, *minato-ku, japan*
Canadian High Commission, *singapore*
High Commission of the Democratic Socialist
   Republic of Sri Lanka, *singapore*
Embassy of the Czech Republic, *singapore*
Embassy of the Republic of Panama, *singapore*
Royal Embassy of Saudi Arabia, *singapore*
Embassy of the Slovak Republic, *jakarta, indonesia*
Embassy of the Republic of Croatia,
   jakarta, indonesia

Embassy of Ghana, *tokyo, japan*
High Commission of the Republic of Zimbabwe,
   canberra, australia
High Commission of Brunei Darussalam, *singapore*
Embassy of the Russian Federation, *singapore*
Embassy of the United Arab Emirates,
   jakarta, indonesia
High Commission for the Islamic Republic
   of Pakistan, *singapore*
Embassy of Guatemala, *tokyo, japan*
Embassy of Greece, *bangkok, thailand*
Embassy of the Republic of Tunisia, *jakarta, indonesia*
The Pamodzi Hotel, *lusaka, zambia*
Embassy of Israel, *singapore*
Embassy of Lebanon, *tokyo, japan*
Slovenian Tourist Board, *ljublhana*
Antigua Department of Tourism and Trade,
   toronto, canada
Monaco Government Tourist Office, *u.s.a.*
Seychelles Tourism Marketing Authority,
   seychelles, africa
Embassy of the Republic of Cote d'Ivoire,
   tokyo, japan
High Commission of the Independent State of
   Papua New Guinea, *singapore*
Embassy of the Republic of El Salvador, *tokyo, japan*
Belize Tourism Board, *belize, central america*
Bahamas Ministry of Tourism, *bahama*
Australian High Commission, *singapore*
Embassy of the Republic of Austria, *singapore*
Permanent Mission of Antigua and Barbuda,
   new york, u.s.a.
Embassy of the People's Republic of China, *singapore*
Embassy of the Republic of Indonesia, *singapore*
Embassy of Burkina Faso, *tokyo, japan*
Embassy of the Federative Republic Of Brazil, *singapore*
Embassy of Finland, *singapore*
Embassy of the Republic of Hungary, *singapore*
Royal Netherlands Embassy, *singapore*
Royal Norwegian Embassy, *singapore*
Embassy of The Republic of Philippines, *singapore*
Embassy of Sweden, *singapore*
Cyprus Tourism Organisation
Permanent Mission of the Republic of Estonia
   to the United Nations, *new york, u.s.a.*
Embassy of the Union of Myanmar, *singapore*
Consulate General of Iceland, *singapore*
Singapore Tourism Board, *singapore*

We would also like to extend our gratitude to the following sponsors whose donations have made this publication possible.

Immortal The Design Station Pte Ltd, *singapore*
Michael Khoo Hong Chin, *singapore*
Goldcom Investment Co Ltd, *hong kong*
American Restaurant Group, *u.s.a.*
Andrew Kwek Tse Hock, *singapore*
National Library Board, *singapore*
Long Kee Investment Co Ltd, *hong kong*
Rockreef Investment Ltd, *hong kong*
The Fullerton Singapore, *singapore*
Mr and Mrs Peter Chua, *singapore*
Chesterton International Property Consultants Pte Ltd, *singapore*
Singapore Power Ltd, *singapore*
Man Sun Long Co Ltd, *hong kong*
Techwah Printing & Packaging Pte Ltd, *singapore*
Tung Hsing Transfer Printing Co.Ltd, *taiwan*
Si Chong Investment Co Ltd, *hong kong*
The Magic of ChongQing Hot Pot Pte Ltd, *singapore*
Superbowl – The Art of Eating Congee Pte Ltd, *singapore*
De Cheng Xin Xing Trading Pte Ltd, *singapore*
Pacific International Lines Pte Ltd, *singapore*
John Chionh, *pakistan*
Ng, Lee & Associates – DFK, *singapore*
Jeanette Yong Nyet Ngoh, *singapore*
Win & Win Pte Ltd, *singapore*
Singapore Sangchoy Colour Separation Pte Ltd, *singapore*
Singapore Turf Club, *singapore*
Farina Wijaya, *indonesia*
Chinese Feasts Pte Ltd, *singapore*
Suntec City Development Pte Ltd, *singapore*
Lim Ai Hia, *malaysia*
Oser Design Pte Ltd, *singapore*
Pigeonman Trading, *singapore*
Leonard Soh Hee Chuan, *singapore*
Lucky Square Pte Ltd, *singapore*
Tak Cheung Travel Pte Ltd, *singapore*
Wendy Wong & Partners, *singapore*
Wong Chui Kit, *singapore*
SICC Singapore Ladies Golfer, *singapore*

We acknowledge the commemorative plates presented by World Kitchen (Asia Pacific) Pte Ltd, *singapore*.

introduction

The globalisation of economies and ideas have rendered borders – political as well as cultural – secondary to international understanding and camaraderie. People from all walks of life, from all corners of the world, are, today, united through the Internet as well as a host of other technologically aided avenues. But as science and technology take mankind beyond the boundaries of the familiar, one aspect has stood the test of time. Regardless of race or religion, the food we eat will always reflect who we really are.

Since time immemorial, the food on our tables has been a function of many different attributes. Some argue that what we eat is dependent on what is available. Others portend that our beliefs shape the nature of our cuisine. One thing is for certain, food invariably means more to us than mere sustenance.

It is there to not only to appease hunger, but also to celebrate victory, or to signify a religious event. It is a show of warmth and generosity, and an extension of hospitality to our neighbours and fellow man. At times, it is even there to acknowledge the inevitability of death and, perhaps, the passing on to another world. As important as food is to our very existence, it is very often used to define what kind of existence.

This book had its beginnings in 1995 when Jeannie Lau, then in the food business, visited a Singaporean friend in New York. Over a good meal and fine wine, the conversation, as is customary of Singaporeans, drifted to food. Jeannie's friend threw up the idea of gathering recipes from all the countries in the United Nations and compiling them into a book. It sounded like a fine idea to Jeannie at the time, but just an idea, nevertheless.

Half a decade later, Jeannie Lau used the impetus from this very idea to return to the publishing industry. She set up Milestone-Millennium Press in Singapore in 1999 and began to realise a dream that had its roots five years before. At the turn of this new century, *An Assembly of Tastes – The Culinary World of the United Nations*, was born.

The premise of *An Assembly of Tastes – The Culinary World of the United Nations* is as diplomatic as the tenets of the United Nations. Each UN country was approached, through either their embassies or tourism boards, to offer recipes that they deemed representative of their heritage. Together with comprehensive research and a series of interviews with individuals, Milestone-Millennium Press pieced together this compendium of global food culture. In return for the kindness, time and effort extended by all embassies and tourism offices around the world, the net proceeds of this book will be donated to UNIFEM, and the Kidney Dialysis Foundation of Singapore. It is a small way for us to help two worthy charities face the challenges of the new millennium.

There are, as of the date of publication, 189 countries in the United Nations. Trying to apportion space to each of them was one of our main challenges. We have tried our best to ensure that all 189 entities are mentioned in one way or form. We apologise if we have not been able to include recipes from every single country, and would like to assure everyone that this shortcoming is purely logistic in nature, and bears no prejudice whatsoever.

The main goal of this book is to provide a high quality collector's piece that will open the minds, and palates, of the reader to our wonderfully varied world of food. As we cross over to a new era in history, more than ever, the idea of fellowship, tolerance and acceptance for each other's historical and cultural backgrounds are ultimately important in preserving our future as a world at peace. There is little doubt that the way to most people's hearts is through their stomachs. If that is the case, we hope to foster a new world of understanding through this international ensemble.

Tan Ju Kuang, *editor*

our beneficiaries

This compendium of culinary diversity is a reflection of the many cultures making up our world. Awareness is often the first step to acceptance. In this case, acceptance of another's beliefs, culture and way of life. In many ways, charity is a form of acceptance – an acknowledgement, if you will, that there are those around who are not as privileged. As Milestone-Millennium's inaugural sojourn to the world of publishing, all net proceeds from the sale of our first run will be donated to two charities: the Kidney Dialysis Foundation in Singapore and UNIFEM.

The Kidney Dialysis Foundation (KDF) of Singapore is a non-profit organisation established in February 1996 with the support of the Ministry of Health of Singapore. KDF provides subsidized haemodialysis treatment only to the needy members of the Singapore community. All patients receiving treatment from the KDF are referred by the medical social workers in the hospitals.

The mission of KDF is to provide high quality, low cost treatment to needy patients in Singapore; provide patient support services to all kidney patients in Singapore; promote public awareness and education on kidney diseases to members of the Singapore public; conduct education programmes for healthcare givers and medical professionals; and conduct clinical research on kidney diseases.

KDF operates two dialysis centres in Singapore and offers treatment to over 160 patients. The Foundation supports its operations from a subsidy from the Ministry of Health and from the public through its many fund-raising projects and events.

UNIFEM was established as an innovative and catalytic fund for women's empowerment and gender equality. UNIFEM supports innovative and experimental activities benefiting women in line with national and regional priorities. It serves as a catalyst, with the goal of ensuring the appropriate involvement of women in mainstream development activities, as often as possible at the pre-investment stage. UNIFEM plays an innovative and catalytic role in relation to the United Nations' overall system of development cooperation.

UNIFEM is the women's fund at the United Nations that provides financial support and technical assistance to innovative programmes promoting women's human rights, their economic and political empowerment, and gender equality. It advocates within the UN system to link women's interests and concerns to all critical issues on the national, regional and global agendas. UNIFEM is an autonomous organisation working in close association with the United Nations Development Programme (UNDP).

UNIFEM focuses on three areas of immediate concern: strengthening women's economic rights and empowering them to enjoy secure livelihoods; engendering governance and leadership that increase women's participation in the decision-making processes that shape their lives; and promoting women's human rights to eliminate all forms of violence against women and transform development into a more peaceful, equitable and sustainable process.

UNIFEM is dedicated to building stronger women's organisations and networks so that women themselves have the power to negotiate new and better policies with their governments and international agencies. It provides technical support to governments, and promotes dialogue between them and women's organisations. In the context of the Secretary-General's UN reform agenda, UNIFEM supports the UN system in ensuring that gender concerns are incorporated into the policies and activities of UN organisations, governments, and civil society partners.

foreword by professor tommy koh, ambassador at large, ministry of foreign affairs, singapore

I am truly delighted to write the foreword to this lovely book. I do so not only because, as Minister George Yeo once said, "food is the Tao of Singapore". All Singaporeans love good food. The variety, quality and affordability of good food is one of the glories of Singapore.

I congratulate Mrs Jeannie Lau and Dr Philip Chin for conceptualizing this book and for bringing it to fruition. I congratulate them for publishing this book for three reasons.

First, I believe that food, like music, unites the human family. During the past thirty years, the world has become increasingly cosmopolitan. One of the evidence for this trend is the proliferation of restaurants which serve cuisines from around the world in our towns and cities. There is no danger that the whole world will be hooked on hamburgers. Chinese, Indian, Japanese, Thai, Vietnamese and other Asian cuisines have traveled successfully to the four corners of the world. In the same way, Asians have acquired a taste for the cuisines of Europe, North and South America, and the Middle East.

Second, I believe that enjoying the food of another country can open a window into another civilisation. Let me cite Japanese cuisine as an example. I love Japanese food. Through my love of Japanese food I have been motivated to learn more about Japanese history and culture. I have also come to admire Japanese aesthetics, which is manifested in the manner in which Japanese food is prepared and presented.

Third, I believe that great chefs are great artists. Cooking is a culinary art. Like other forms of art, one has to be born with a talent for cooking. This talent has then to be honed by years of training and practice. How often have you tasted a dish or a meal and felt that the person who had prepared it is an artist? I have often done so. It need not be an expensive meal. It need not be a complicated dish. It can be a fish steamed to perfection. It can be the humble "wonton" noodle. It can be Singapore's irresistible Chili Crab. When I taste perfection I know that it is the creation of a master artist. Let me therefore take this opportunity to salute the chefs of the world.

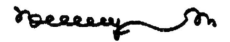

Professor Tommy Koh, *ambassador-at-large, ministry of foreign affairs*

AN ASSEMBLY OF TASTES

the culinary world of the united nations

a milestone-millennium press publication

contents

asia

NORTH ASIA 1 CHINA 2 MONGOLIA

3 REPUBLIC OF KOREA

4 DEMOCRATIC PEOPLE'S

REPUBLIC OF KOREA 5 JAPAN

CENTRAL ASIA 6 KAZAKHSTAN

7 KYRGYZSTAN 8 TAJIKISTAN

9 TURKMENISTAN 10 UZBEKISTAN

SOUTHERN ASIA 11 BRUNEI DARUSSALAM

12 CAMBODIA 13 INDONESIA

14 LAO PEOPLE'S DEMOCRATIC REPUBLIC

15 MALAYSIA 16 MYANMAR 17 PHILIPPINES

18 SINGAPORE 19 THAILAND

20 VIETNAM 21 INDIA 22 BANGLADESH

WEST ASIA 23 AFGHANISTAN

24 BHUTAN 25 NEPAL 26 PAKISTAN

27 MALDIVES 28 SRI LANKA

china

From the highland of the Tibetan plateaus to the lower reaches of the Yangtze river delta, geographical diversity has given birth to a wealth of culinary styles in China. Food here is also greatly influenced by the hundreds of races, dialectic groups, and religious persuasions of its people. However, broadly speaking, cooking styles in this country, which has a land mass equivalent in size to the United States of America, may be divided into four main schools: the Peking or Northern School; the Shanghai or Eastern School; the Sichuan or Western School; and the Canton or Southern School.

The Northern School is a dichotomous one. Home of Beijing and the Imperial Palace, some of the most elaborate cuisines hail from this region. Peking duck, for one, is a popular northern dish that is known for its elaborate preparation and elegant presentation. On the other hand, the land up north is harsh. Winters are frigidly cold, and summers are hot and humid. As a result, simple dishes like firepot represent an easy to assemble meal that warms more than the senses when the temperature dips.

The sea on one side and fertile land on the other, it is little wonder that the Eastern School thrives in this 'land of fish and rice'. Cooking found here is also known as the Huaiyang School of the Yangtse River Delta. The fertile lands of Anhui and Jiangsu provinces make this one of China's leading agricultural regions. Wheat, rice, barley, corn, sweet potatoes and peanuts are grown widely, featuring in many of the dishes from this part of China. As the culinary centre of the Eastern School, Shanghai cooking is characterised by its exquisite appearance, richness, and a penchant for the sweet.

fire pot lamb

1 De-vein and de-bone the lamb, then cut into very thin slices. Set on a serving plate. 2 Mix together all dipping sauce ingredients. 3 Pour enough stock to fill the fire pot. Bring to a boil. 4 Put in the cabbage and mung bean noodles to cook. 5 Dip the lamb slices into the sugar-garlic mixture then into the soup to cook. Once cooked to desired doneness, take out and dip into sauce before eating. The same may be done with the cooked cabbage and noodles. 6 Serve with steamed white rice.

750 g lamb
500 g cabbage
  cut into coarse shreds
1 – 2 cups transparent mung
  bean noodles, soaked in cold
  water till soft
2 tbsp garlic minced and mixed
  with a little sugar
stock for cooking
steamed white rice

dipping sauce (per serving)
1 tbsp sesame paste
1 tsp pickled chives, chopped
1 tsp fermented bean curd
1 tsp soya sauce
1 tsp chili sauce
1 tsp shrimp oil
1 tsp sesame oil
1 tsp Shaoxing wine

The Sichuan basin is one of the richest lands in China. The relative inaccessibility of this region – Tang Dynasty poet Li Po said that 'it is harder to get to Sichuan than to heaven' – helped it develop a most distinctive cooking style. Rich, piquant tasting food found here is influenced by its neighbouring regions of Hunan and Guizhou. Chengdu is Sichuan's culinary capital, while Chongqing is famous for its hot pot cuisine. Among the Western School, Sichuan dishes are known to possess a range of conflicting flavours – sweet, sour, bitter, hot, salty, fragrant – all combining to form a complex but most delicious concoction.

The Cantonese School, or Southern School, is undoubtedly the most famous of all Chinese cooking styles. Arguably, authentic Cantonese food has no rival in its variety, and its breadth and popularity extend far and wide. Rice is the dominant staple in this region. Other crops are tea, tobacco, sugar cane and sub-tropical fruits like bananas, oranges and lychees. Hainan Island in the south is the only place in China that grows coconuts and rubber.

Within the Southern School are three regional styles: Canton, Chaochow and Dong Jiang. The Cantonese style is known for its creativity, the Chaochow for its seafood, and the Dong Jiang for its richness. The Dong Jiang school is part of the *Hakka* (meaning 'guest') people who are immigrants from north China who settled here after the Mongol invasion in the thirteenth century.

FOOD AS THERAPY

For the Chinese, life is a careful balance of opposites. Yin and yang are two equal opposing elements that hold the universe, as well as our bodies, in healthy harmony. And as far as our physiological well-being is concerned, there is no better way to affect this equilibrium than through the foods which we put through our mouths. The elaborate preparation and display of Chinese dishes are well documented. But what escape the laymen's eyes are the unique therapeutic qualities inherent in many common ingredients, at least as far as the Chinese believe.

MUNGBEAN VERMICELLI

This clear, cellophane-like noodle is known to 'cool' the body (i.e. yin) and is good for expectant mothers at the last stages of pregnancies, especially in hot weather. Mung bean vermicelli is often used in place of noodles in soups.

BLACK CHICKEN

Used in many Chinese tonic soups with an assortment of herbs, it is a yang food, i.e. 'heaty' in nature. It is good for anaemia and women recovering from childbirth. In general, it strengthens one's overall constitution.

LOTUS ROOT

Often used in soups, and sometimes pickled, lotus root has always been looked upon highly by the Chinese for its ability to purify the blood system and 'lubricate' the lungs.

GINGKO NUTS

The wonders of gingko have recently taken over the West with its purported enhancement of brain activity. The Chinese also believe that it is good for coughs with lots of phlegm, and for cleaning the urinary tract. Gingko nuts are used in many soup or sauce-based dishes, as well as in desserts.

150 g chicken breast, cut into
  thin shreds
25 g pickled chilies
100 g bamboo shoot, cut into
  small strips
25 g celery, cut into small strips
1½ tsp cornstarch
2 tsp vinegar
2 tbsp scallions, chopped
1 tbsp fresh ginger, shredded
2 cloves garlic, sliced
1 cup cooking wine
salt, pepper, water
3 tbsp peanut oil
steamed white rice

fried chicken with pickled chilies (sichuan)

1 Mix ½ tsp of the cornstarch with about half a cup of water, then blend well into the shredded chicken breast. **2** Mix the rest of the cornstarch with the cooking wine, a pinch of salt and pepper, and vinegar in a bowl to make a sauce. **3** Heat about 3 tbsp of peanut oil in a wok. Fry the chicken, then the scallion, ginger, garlic slices and pickled chilies. **4** Stir fry for about 3 – 5 minutes, then drop in the bamboo shoot and celery. Fry for another 2 minutes, then pour in the sauce. Fry a little more until the sauce thickens. **5** Serve with steamed white rice.

boiled crucian carp with clam (shanghai)

1 Clean the carps. Then prepare the fish by cutting a shallow slit along the backbone and making several cuts on the sides. **2** Put in a saucepan with cold water (just enough to submerse the fish), and season with salt, ginger slices, scallion sections, and bamboo shoots. Boil over low heat till done. Transfer the fish onto to a soup plate; set aside the fish soup. **3** Drop the clams into a saucepan; cover with cold water. Bring to a boil until the shells open. Remove the clams then extract the meat into a bowl. **4** Strain the fish soup, then add to the clam stock and bring to a boil. **5** Add mushrooms and ham, then season with salt and pour over the fish in the soup plate.

2 crucian carps
250 g live clams
3 slices of ham
5 slices of bamboo shoot
1 Chinese mushroom,
  soaked, then sliced
2 tbsp ginger slices
½ cup scallions, cut into
  5-cm sections
salt to taste

steamed spare ribs in black bean sauce (canton)

1 Chop spareribs into small pieces. **2** Mince finely the garlic, ginger root and red chili. Mix the marinade ingredients. **3** Marinate the spare ribs with this marinade mixture for 15 minutes. **4** Grease a heat-proof plate with oil; place spareribs on it; steam vigorously for 25 – 30 minutes. **5** Garnish with scallions and serve.

750 g pork spareribs, cut into
  small pieces
2 cloves garlic, crushed
1 5-cm piece ginger root, peeled
1 tsp oil
1 small fresh red chili

marinade
2 tbsp black bean sauce
1 tbsp soya sauce
1 tbsp rice wine or sherry
1 tsp cornstarch

garnish
2 scallions cut into short lengths

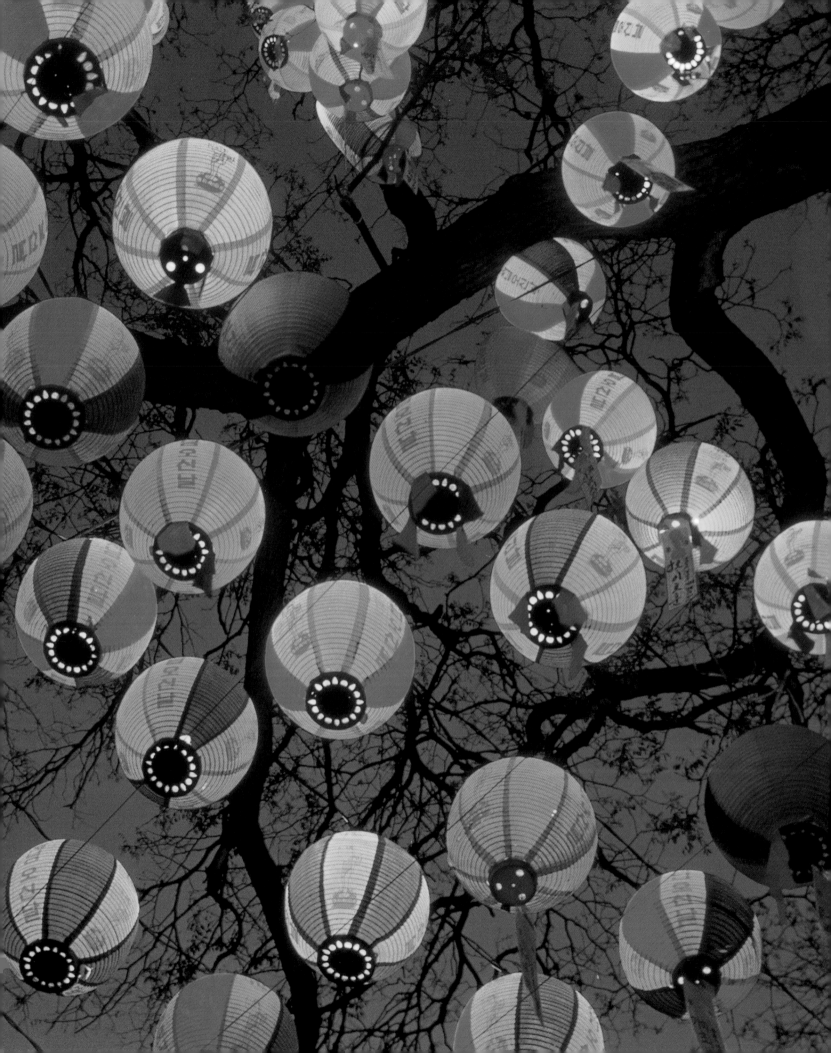

korea

Like many countries in Asia, food in Korea is more than just a means of subsistence; it is a way of life. Great emphasis is placed on the taste, appearance, and just as significantly, the balance of a meal – nutritionally or otherwise.

For Koreans, a meal is incomplete without their beloved *kim chee*. Based on the pickling of either Chinese cabbage or white radish, there exists more than 200 varieties. In its many forms – as is, in soups, pancakes, or even in a sandwich – *kim chee* is eaten at breakfast, lunch, and dinner. The affinity towards this salty, spicy and sour item may be entrenched in the preference of pungent tastes. This pungency is deemed necessary for stimulating appetite.

The presence of chili pepper is just as ubiquitous in Korean food. This is interesting if you consider the fact that the chili originated half a world away in the Americas. Reportedly, Portuguese priests who traveled with the Japanese troops introduced chili seeds to the country during the Japan-Korea war in the 16th century. Its popularity caught on like wild fire and chilies are now a staple in every household.

Korea is a country steeped in the philosophies of Confucianism and Buddhism. These beliefs are conveyed in their attitude towards food. For one, Koreans like to eat their meals with all dishes laid out on the table at the same time. A range of side dishes – consisting of, perhaps, *kim chee* (naturally), blanched spinach, cooked bean sprouts or fried anchovies – also characterises a typical Korean spread. Koreans believe that this confluence of colours and tastes symbolises the harmonious balance between heaven, earth and man.

2 kg beef, thinly sliced
steamed white rice

seasoning sauce
1 cup soya sauce
½ cup sugar
½ cup honey
1 cup red wine
3 tbsp garlic, chopped
4 tbsp green onions, chopped
1 tbsp black pepper
2 tbsp sesame oil

bulgogi

1 Mix the ingredients for the sauce together. **2** Dip the beef, piece by piece, in the seasoning sauce. Place meat in a plastic container and let marinate for at least 2 hours. **3** Drain the beef of excess marinade and grill over a griddle or broil in an oven till cooked. **4** Serve with steamed white rice.

japan

With minimalism emerging as a definitive trend of the last decade, it is no wonder that Japanese cuisine has reached epic popularity all over the world. *Sushi* and *sashimi* – the raw fish delicacies once considered outlandish in the West – have now become a staple in every major city, and *teppanyaki* counters and noodle bars are sighted everywhere.

Part of the huge popularity of Japanese food must be attributed to its nutritional value – most dishes are seasoned lightly and cooked simply. With food low in fat and cholesterol and high in mineral-rich seafood and seaweeds, the Japanese live longer than anyone else in the world and have startlingly low incidences of heart disease.

However, for the Japanese, perfectly cooked, healthy food of the finest quality isn't enough. A dish must transcend practicality into art – the appearance of food is as important as its flavour. No detail is overlooked. For instance, a *kaiseki* meal may have more than 15 or 20 dishes made from the finest ingredients, each harmoniously balanced on exquisite china or elegant lacquer dishes.

The art of Japanese food can be witnessed even at the most casual of *sushi* bars. Walk into one and marvel at the dexterity of knife-wielding *sushi* chefs, who prepare their specialities with awe-inspiring artistry. This penchant for perfectionism also means *tempura* restaurants only serve *tempura* (seafood and vegetables deep-fried in fluffy batter) while others specialise in *sukiyaki* (a meat fondue) or in *o-konomiyaki* (pancake with vegetables or seafood cooked by the customer on a hotplate). *Fugu* (blowfish) restaurants prepare this fish, whose liver contains a fatal toxin, in a hundred different ways. *Fugu* is considered a luxury albeit a dangerous one.

The iconoclastic rice wine, *sake*, features at any true Japanese meal. Served hot or cold, *sake* from different regions in the country have their own distinctive tastes. Nada, near Kobe, produces one with a strong clean flavor, while that from the Kyoto region is more delicate.

Green tea is also drunk in large quantities and has a subtler flavour compared to fermented black teas. The Japanese tea ceremony, introduced by Zen Buddhist monks, uses the finest quality green tea and emphasises the aesthetics of the room and the utensils as essential aspects of the ceremony. Like much of Japanese cuisine, this gracious, mannered ceremony extends beyond a mere culinary experience to become an aesthetic and even spiritual ritual.

sushi vinegar
   (1 part vinegar to 3 parts water),
   5 cups rice (short grain type),
   cooked 8 sheets *nori* (roasted laver),
   cut into bite-size pieces

sushi fillings
fish fillet, raw and fresh tuna, squid,
   sea bream, vegetable cucumber,
   avocado

seasonings
wasabi (japanese horse radish)
gari (pickled ginger)

temaki zushi (hand-rolled sushi)

1 Put cooked rice in a bowl and mix *sushi* vinegar into the rice. Wait for it to cool down to room temperature. **2** Place the rice evenly on a sheet of *nori* with one to three of the *sushi* ingredients on it, put a pinch of *wasabi* and wrap it to form a *temaki zushi*. **3** If you wish, you can have as many varieties as you want for raw *sushi* fillings, such as *uni* (sea urchin), *ikura* (salmon roe), prawn and crab.

soviet central asia

kazakhstan.turkmenistan.tajikistan.kyrgyzstan.uzbekistan

Soviet Central Asia is undeniably one of the most ethnically diverse areas on our planet. As the hub of some of the earliest civilisations in the region, the cuisine here is accented with flavours from both the eastern and western world.

Even though a visit to any market in Central Asia will unravel inevitable similarities, on closer inspection, culinary distinctions do occur among the countries. The diet of the people in Turkmenistan comprises mostly meat from camels, horses, lamb, *dzeiran* (mountain goat), and milk products. *Kavardak* (lamb, flavoured with a herb from the *saksul* plant, cooked in claypots) is a national delicacy, and so are mung bean porridge and a tasty, meatless *pilaf*. For those who live along the Caspian Sea, fish like sturgeon, whitefish and snapper often find their way into soups, *pilafs*, *kebabs*, and fish dumplings like the delightful *balik borek*. The nomadic people of Kazakhstan and Kyrgyzstan often subsist on very simple food. Staples in their diet include boiled meats, especially lamb, horse and *kazi* (spiced horse-meat sausage). *Besh barmak* (literally means "five fingers" as it is eaten with the hand) is a popular dish of homemade noodles cooked with lamb and served with a broth. Large amounts of milk products and bread are also consumed in this part of the region.

The cuisines of Tajikistan and Uzbekistan are often considered the most refined in Central Asia, as these republics are deeply influenced by the Persians, Chinese, Afghani, and even the Indians. Vegetables, chickpeas and lentils are commonly used in their cooking – steaming being the preferred method of preparation. Rice *pilaf* is a common favourite, as is *tahum barak* (egg-filled *ravioli* coated with sesame oil). Other signature dishes include *manti* (large spicy lamb dumplings), *samsa* (walnut-filled pastries) and *kuk samsa* (pastries filled with scallions or herbs). Tea without milk is drunk universally and alcohol is consumed despite their Muslim inclination.

pais daging

1 Cut beef into tiny cubes, wash and strain. **2** Mix *sago* with a little water and strain. **3** Mix together all the ingredients and leave for 15 minutes. **4** Wrap mixture in *pucuk* leaves, and secure it with the vein of a coconut leaf or a heat-proof string. **5** Grill over moderate heat till cooked.

600 g beef
3 shallots
2 garlic cloves
1 tsp pepper
1 tbsp *sago*
salt and sugar to taste
***pucuk* leaves to wrap**
    (a type of indigenous
    heat-proof leaf)

brunei darussalam

Talk of the Sultanate's riches often distracts one's attention away from the culinary highlights of this small (Australia's Northern Territories is larger than the whole country), but affluent nation. Sharing a landmass with East Malaysia, food in Brunei reflects many similarities with its Islamic neighbour.

Rice is the staple foundation from which most meals are built. Like many Southeast Asian countries, the preference is for the fiery, and spicy dishes are certainly more a norm than the exception. Coconut, in one form or another is frequently used, most pertinently as a base for the curries and spicy vegetables stews that proliferate. And when rice is not present, you can bet that some form of fried noodles will be there to take its place. Seafood, chicken and beef are always popular and are prepared roasted, fried, or braised in a curry.

Like Singapore and Malaysia, the trio of Indian, Chinese and Malay influence has also swayed Bruneian cuisine. Apart from the general acceptance of dishes from these origins (within the context of Islamic acceptance, of course), Chinese and Indian restaurants – as well as Western ones – are a common sight in the capital of Bandar Seri Begawan.

For the most part, fish is the local's main source of protein. The country imports a major portion of its fish intake and regional varieties like *tenggiri* (mackerel), *ikan merah* (red snapper) and *kerapu* (garoupa) are commonly found in local markets. Items that are typically Bruneian tend to be rice-based. *Kalupi* (individually packaged, steamed sweet rice cake), *kueh koci* (rice flour dumplings with sweet coconut filling wrapped in banana leaves), and *cucur ubi* (sweet potato fritters) are but several examples of indigenous creativity.

cambodia

In the last few centuries, the ravages of war have done little to alter the food of the Cambodians. Indeed, given the reach of the Khmer empire from the 9th to the 15th century, one might even suggest a hint of Cambodian influence in the dishes of neighbouring countries like Thailand, Laos and Vietnam.

That having been said, European accents throughout the country today reflect a time in the mid-19th century when it was a colony of France. Bakeries and frog's legs are but two incidences that point to a history of foreign rule.

The Mekong and Tonle Sap rivers provide the lifeline to Cambodia's mainstay of freshwater fish. The industry is so vibrant that it produces enough for export to the region. The heart of Cambodian cuisine is still imbedded in the Southeast Asian practice of eating rice with several communal style dishes. These might include *samlaa* (soup or stew), *chha* (a sautéed dish), *chion* (a fried dish) and *aing* (a grilled dish of meat or fish). Herbs like Asian sweet basil, long-leafed coriander, and a wide variety of mints are often used in each preparation. Even though Cambodians do use chilies like *mteh kraachaak neang* (a thin chili about 15 cm long) and *mteh kmang* (birdseye chili), they use it sparingly compared to their neighbours. And if chilies are used, they are usually eaten as a garnish or dip, not as an ingredient.

samlaa nom ban chiok

Although many Cambodian dishes share similar origins or characteristics with Laotian, Thai, or Vietnamese counterparts, *nom ban chiok* is one that is typical of the Khmer people. It is a kind of noodles made of rice and water. *Nom ban chiok* is eaten in a variety of ways. This particular version comes in a soup made with fish.

Samlaa nom ban chiok is often served during festive periods like the Cambodian New Year, 14th of April. This traditional dish is customarily prepared for friends and relatives who come visiting during this holiday.

Generally speaking, those in the North have a preference for stronger tastes and make their version with more *prahoc*, sugar and lemon.

samlaa: **1** Cook cleaned fish in boiling water. **2** De-bone the cooked fish and set aside. **3** Cut the lemon grass, *lemyit* and *kechiya* into little pieces, pound into a paste. **4** Mix fish meat into the paste. **5** Bring fish stock to a boil again, put the herb/fish mixture into the stock. **6** Put the *prahoc* and coconut milk into the stock, add salt and sugar to taste. **7** In a serving bowl, combine one serving of the *nom ban chiok* with some raw bean sprouts, long beans, ground peanuts and sliced cucumber. **8** Pour the stock (*sam laa*) over the *nom ban chiok*, serve hot. **nom ban chiok:** **1** Put rice in a large pot and cover with water, soak overnight. **2** The next day, sieve rice and grind till it forms a paste and shape into a ball. **3** Bring another pot of water to boil. **4** Cook rice ball in the water for about 1–2 hours. **5** Remove rice balls from the water and pound it further into a paste. **6** Press the rice paste through a special grater called a *paen* or a normal grater with large holes. **7** Put the grated noodles in a bowl of cold water to cool. **8** Cut noodles to required length and form into individual bundles, ready to be used.

nom ban chiok
3 litres of water
1 kg of river fish, such as
  tri rhor, or *tri chrao*
6 stalks of lemon grass
1 5-cm piece of *lemyit*,
  a kind of turmeric
5 5-cm pieces of *kechiya*, an
  indigenous root (found in South-
  east Asian or Thai grocery stores)
1 cup thick coconut milk
2 tbsp *prahoc*, a kind of pungent
  salted fish (found in Southeast
  Asian or Thai grocery stores)
salt and sugar to taste

garnish
bean sprouts
long beans
peanuts, ground
cucumbers, julienned

indonesia

A giant archipelago of over 13,000 islands and nearly 200 million people, Indonesia is a populous country boasting varied tastes derived from its history of Portuguese, English, Dutch, Chinese and Indian influences. In addition to this rich multi-cultural past, numerous racial and tribal groups inhabit the country – each with their very own culinary culture.

In Java, two dishes stand out – *gado-gado* (fresh crisp vegetables in stinging hot peanut sauce, sometimes served with *longtong* (rice cakes), hard-boiled eggs, fried *tempeh* and *krupuk* (deep-fried prawn cracker) or *emping* (deep-fried cracker made from the *belinjo* nut), and *gudeg*, a traditional Yogya one-dish meal. It is essentially sweet and comprises jackfruit served with *opor ayam* (similar to curry chicken) and *sambal goreng krecek* (fried and placed on a pile of white boiled rice, topped with *blondo* – a very thick white creamed coconut).

In Bali, you may enjoy the rather laid-back atmosphere and tasty food found in *warungs* (eating houses). Savour their *babi guling* (suckling pig roasted whole over a pit), only in Bali, as it is here where the predominantly Islamic country's Hindus primarily reside. In nearby Lombok, you can sample the *sate sumsum* (a *kebab*-style dish made of bone marrow).

A visit at lunchtime to Sulawesi (historically Celebes) would enable you to sample their *panada* (an appetizer); a chilli-hot fish soup; *pakis* (young fernshoots) in hot chili; and *ayam rica rica* (a grilled chicken) served with white rice. You may then quench your burning throat with *saguer*, an unfermented juice from coconut flowers. On visiting the Spice Islands (renowned for its cloves and nutmeg), try their *terung goreng dengan saus santan* (fried aubergines with coconut milk sauce) and *ikan asam pedis* (hot and sour fish).

nasi kuning with meatballs in coconut sauce and fried chicken livers

This dish has long been used to celebrate milestone events in an Indonesian household. A birthday, a baby's first haircut, the first seven months of a pregnancy and a child's first steps, these are just some significant events where *nasi kuning*, or 'yellow rice', is served. There are many kinds of dishes that accompany *nasi kuning* and we have included two with our rice recipe.

nasi kuning: **1** Steam the rice for about 25 minutes until half-cooked, then remove from steamer. **2** Dissolve turmeric in a bit of water, strain the liquid into the coconut milk and add the rest of the ingredients except the lime juice. Heat it to boiling. **3** When boiling, pour the rice into the coconut milk mixture, continue to stir until the rice has absorbed the milk. **4** Remove from the heat, add the lime juice and then steam the rice till cooked (about 1 hour). **meatballs: 1** Mix the beef with salt and egg. Shape into meatballs the size of marbles and then steam for about 15 minutes. Fry the meatballs until golden, remove and set aside. **2** Heat 3 tbsp of oil in frying pan. Fry the pounded spice paste, tomatoes, red chilies, *salam* leaf and *langkuas* until fragrant. **3** Add the shrimps, *terasi*, salt and brown sugar. **4** When the shrimps turn colour, add the coconut milk and the meatballs. Stir occasionally till the coconut milk has evaporated. **chicken livers: 1** Season the chicken livers and hearts with the tamarind, water and salt. Let stand for about 15 minutes. **2** Heat the vegetable oil. Fry the hearts and liver till cooked. Remove and drain on paper towels. **3** Serve skewered using bamboo sticks.

nasi kuning

1½ kg long grain rice,
   washed and drained
1 ½ tbsp fresh turmeric, grated
2¼ litre coconut milk, from
   1½ coconuts
3 stalks lemon grass, bruised
4 *salam* leaves
4 kaffir lime leaves
2 tbsp lime juice
salt to taste

meatballs

500 g ground beef
1 egg
2 tomatoes, chopped
6 red chilies, sliced
1 *salam* leaf
1 cm fresh *langkuas* (also
   known as *galangal* or
   blueginger), bruised
1 slice *terasi*
250 g shrimps, peeled
375 ml coconut milk from
   ½ coconut, a pinch of brown
   sugar or palm sugar

spice paste

10 shallots
4 cloves of garlic
10 red chilies
oil for frying

chicken livers

20 chicken livers
20 chicken hearts
1 tsp tamarind dissolved in
   1 tbsp water
salt to taste
vegetable oil
bamboo skewers

chicken laab

A key ingredient of any *laab* dish is the fried glutinous rice powder. This is made by frying uncooked glutinous rice in a pan without oil. Once browned and fragrant, the rice is pounded into a powder, ready for use. *Laab* is almost always eaten communally. Often friends and family come together to mix the ingredients in a large communal bowl, chanting, "we are so lucky, we are so lucky" before tucking in.

1 Cook chicken meat in boiling water. **2** De-bone cooked chicken and shred into tiny pieces. **3** Dry the chicken meat and then fry in a hot pan, without oil, till fragrant. Set aside. **4** Mix the chopped chicken and all the other ingredients in a large bowl. **5** Add fish sauce and salt to taste. **6** Serve with sticky rice.

lao people's democratic republic

After decades of colonial rule and intermittent warfare, Lao is finally in a state of peace. Travellers can now visit a land deemed most natural to its Southeast Asian roots. Three quarters of the country is still covered by forests and mountains, and this is reflected in the natural state of Lao cuisine. Food of the Lao is often prepared simply, relying on the uniqueness and freshness of the ingredients to give it character. Lemon grass and fresh coriander are just two of the many herbs that are used, and lime juice is a common agent to give dishes the preferred tang.

At the foundation of every meal is sticky rice. Made by steaming glutinous rice in a special container that resembles an inverted rattan hat, it is customarily eaten with three fingers of one hand. Accompanying dishes of vegetable, poultry, beef or water buffalo are often prepared with a combination of garlic, mint, ground peanuts, ginger and coconut milk – ingredients also common in neighbouring Thailand, Vietnam and Cambodia.

Vegetables eaten in Lao are, however, unique. The Lao people prefer to rummage the forests for wild vegetables. The raw bitterness of these forages is particularly well suited, they feel, to the many different sauces they conjure. These may vary from something as simple as ground chilies, to more exotic ones made from the hide of buffaloes.

If there is one national dish of the Lao, it has to be *laab*. Typically, it is composed of meat (chicken, beef, fish, or prawns) – cooked or, in some instances, raw – tossed with raw vegetables and spiked with hot chilies and lime juice. In a country where meat was difficult to come by, *laab* is often served in celebration of a significant event like birthdays or festivals. The word itself means "good luck" and symbolizes honor, goodwill and happiness.

1 kg chicken meat
4 tbsp lime juice
½ cup banana flour, chopped
½ cup spring onions, chopped
2 tbsp lemon grass, chopped
2 tbsp young ginger, chopped
1 cup fresh bean sprouts
5 small chilies, chopped
2 tbsp fried glutinous rice powder
4 – 6 tbsp chicken stock, or to taste
½ cup chinese parsley
½ cup mint leaves
fish sauce and salt to taste
sticky rice

malaysia

Migrants from other parts of Asia have made Malaysia a melting pot of cultures. Although the country is predominantly Islamic, the prevalence of Christianity, Buddhism, and Hinduism have influenced the culinary make up of this Southeast Asian nation. The country comprises East Malaysia (made up of Sabah and Sarawak on the island of Borneo), and West, or Peninsular, Malaysia. Lush vegetation and a suitable climate have helped the country's export crops of pineapples, palm oil and coconut.

Food in Malaysia is mostly Malay in origin with some influence by the Chinese and Indian migrants. As with most of Asia, rice is a staple, and is usually accompanied by a variety of dishes. Rice variants like *nasi kunyit* (turmeric rice), *nasi goreng* (fried rice) and *nasi lemak* (coconut rice) are often the foil for spicy courses like chicken curry, *prawn sambal* (prawn fried with a spicy sauce), or *sayur lodeh* (curried vegetables). Apart from rice, noodles or *mee* is also a national favourite, and the varieties transcend the different cultures. Malaysian Indians have *mee goreng* (yellow noodles fried with chili sauce, and ketchup); the indigenous Malays have *mee soto* (noodles in chicken soup); and the Chinese have *fried prawn mee* (noodles fried with prawns in a thick brown sauce).

A perfect example of the marriage of different cultures is Malaysia's *Peranakan* community, found mainly in the cities of Melaka and Penang. Born of immigrant Chinese and indigenous Malay lineages, this group of people have their own unique food. *Babi buah keluak* (pork braised with *buah keluak* nuts), *itek tim* (duck soup), and *ikan assam pedas* (fish in tamarind soup) are just some examples of how different cultures can come together in a wonderfully delicious culinary blend.

satay with peanut sauce

satay: 1 Cut the meat into cubes, drain and put aside. 2 Grind coriander, cumin, turmeric, peanuts, cinnamon, shallots and 1 tbsp cooking oil. 3 Marinate meat with this mixture, add sugar and salt to taste. 4 Pierce 5 pieces of meat on one skewer, *kebab* style. 5 Grill *satay* over burning coal, constantly sprinkling cooking oil over the meat using crushed lemon grass stalk. 6 Turn the *satay* over to grill until completely cooked. **sauce:** 1 Grind lemon grass, ginger, and *galangal* until fine. 2 Fry onions until soft, then add pounded chilies. 3 Add tamarind juice, lastly add the peanuts, sugar and salt. 4 Simmer until gravy thickens. 5 Serve *satay* with the sauce separately in a bowl, and with cucumber slices, onion slices and rice cakes.

satay
750 g chicken or beef, de-boned
½ tbsp cumin
¼ tbsp powdered cinnamon
4 shallots, diced
½ tbsp coriander
1 3-cm piece fresh turmeric
1 tsp sugar
½ stalk lemon grass
1 tbsp roasted peanuts
salt to taste
2 tbsp oil

peanut sauce
150 g roasted peanuts, ground finely
1 3-cm piece ginger
1 ½ tbsp chilies, pounded
1 stalk lemon grass
½ onion, sliced
½ cup sugar
½ cup tamarind juice
½ piece of *galangal* (blue ginger)
salt to taste

garnish
1 cucumber, sliced
2 onions, sliced
5 pieces compressed rice cake

mok hinga

This richly flavoured fish soup served over fresh rice noodles and enlivened with an array of spicy accompaniments is considered a Myanmar national dish. The soup is the main feature of the dish, thus, only a small portion of noodles is served in proportion to it.

1 Boil fish in 3 litres of water until tender, de-bone cooked fish and let cool. **2** Mix rice flour and the *dal* powder together with the rest of the water. **3** Strain this mixture into the fish stock and bring to boil, stirring constantly. **4** Clean lemon grass and cut away the tips, put the remaining base of the stalk into the soup. **5** Blend the onions, garlic and ginger. **6** Heat oil in a wok, fry the processed onions, garlic and ginger, add turmeric and stir constantly. **7** Once onions start to brown, add the chili paste and fry until colour deepens. **8** Add the de-boned fish and continue to fry until the fish becomes slightly crispy. Remove from heat. **9** Scoop the fried fish with a slotted spatula, straining the oil, and add to simmering soup. **10** Add the banana stem and continue to cook till stem is tender. **11** Dilute pepper in some water and add to soup. Add fish sauce and salt to taste. Simmer for about 30 minutes. **12** To serve *mok hinga*, place a little cooked rice noodle (*kway teow*) into individual serving bowls. Ladel the rich soup over it. Add sliced eggs, fried shallots, chili powder, lime juice and coriander leaves to garnish.

myanmar

Political upheaval has distracted international attention away from the rich culture, not least of which is culinary, of Myanmar. The former 'Burma', is a peacock-shaped country located between China and India, thus, sharing in the culture and food of both its neighbours.

Economically, Myanmar is a poor nation, but the land abounds with rich vegetation and rivers teem with life. Much of this is reflected in the food the Burmese eat, which may be best described as simple. A lack of modern appliances means that food is often bought on a daily basis. Typically, the best of the country's cuisine is often found in the home, not at restaurants.

The Burmese are passionate about their *mohingar* (fish soup with rice noodles), which is usually eaten at breakfast or at lunchtime. The reputed "national" dish is *ngapi* or *ngapapay* (fermented fish or shrimp paste). It is usually used as a dip or a salad dressing and has a pungent aroma. A typical Burmese meal (usually dinner) is made up of rice and a curry like *ahmai naut* (beef curry) or *whettar sebyan* (pork curry). The perennial favourite soup is *hingyo* (clear soup served with green leafy vegetables), which is served at most meals. Other main courses might include *kyetkaw* (fried chicken), *ngarpaung toke* (fish in banana leaves) or *ahmaithar kyaw* (fried beef), followed by *thakwartlee kyethun chin* (cucumber onion salad) or *syaukthee thoke* (grapefruit salad). Fresh fruits are the norm for dessert and Myanmar produces a copious variety that include mango, jackfruit, papaya and guava. Otherwise, desserts like *kyauk kyaw* (*agar-agar* with coconut) and *sarnwin makin* (semolina cake with coconut) are also popular.

100 g rice flour
100 g *dal* powder
1 kg fish meat, mackerel
500 g onions, coarsely chopped
250 g garlic, coarsely chopped
30 g ginger, finely chopped
6 stalks lemon grass
½ tsp pepper
4 tbsp *nampra* (fish sauce)
salt to taste
1 tbsp chili paste
1 15-cm piece banana stem,
    sliced and soaked briefly
    in water
4 litres water
1 cup oil
½ tsp turmeric powder

accompaniments
lime juice
boiled eggs, sliced
fried shallots
coriander leaves,
    coarsely chopped
fried dried chili powder
kway teow (rice noodle)

philippines

The food of this land is born of indigenous native origins swayed by Spanish and American influences, and an immigration of Chinese flavours. The result is a multi-national heritage that reeks of creativity amidst plurality. For the most part, Filipino food is an intriguing blend of Chinese, Malay and Spanish accents. Rice is the staple of choice and accompanying dishes are often spiked with the mélange of spices commonly found in this part of the world. The multi-purpose coconut provides the foundation of many a dish. The flesh of the fruit may be eaten, as in desserts, or used to produce coconut milk. The juice is fermented to produce intoxicating wines like *tuba* and *lambanog*.

The Chinese, who used the Philippines islands as an early trading center, left a legacy of food influences. Noodles became popular, taking on a new identity called *pansit*. Most notably, Chinese methods of cooking, like steaming, boiling and double-frying, introduced the Filipinos to a brand new world of food preparation. Similarly, Spanish arrival in the 16th century left an indelible imprint. Breads, sausages, barbecued meats and stews in olive oil are part and parcel of the Filipino food map today. Meat dishes with rich sauces like *menudo* and *adobo* are clear reflections of the Spanish legacy.

Understanding the multiplicity of Filipino food requires a closer look at the country itself. The Philippines is lush in natural resources and culturally receptive in attitude, and her inhabitants possess a *joie de vivre* not usually associated with the region. Ultimately, it shows up in the informal and hearty personality of the nation's food.

1 kg chicken thighs
½ cup vinegar
2 tbsp soy sauce
1 clove of garlic, crushed
1 tsp salt
1 tsp ground pepper
½ cups water
1 egg white, beaten
½ cups flour
½ cup cornstarch
½ tsp ground pepper
oil for frying

dip
1 cup mayonnaise
2 cups *adobo* sauce
  (found in Asian grocery
  stores)
2 tbsp parsley, minced
1 tsp garlic, minced

adobong moderno

1 Combine chicken, vinegar, soy sauce, garlic, and half of the salt and pepper in a saucepan. 2 Bring to a boil and then lower heat to simmer. 3 Add the water as the mixture dries, and continue cooking chicken till tender. 4 Remove chicken from pan and strain the remaining sauce. 5 Remove bone from chicken thighs and cut meat in half. 6 Combine flour, cornstarch, and the remainder of the salt and pepper. 7 Dip chicken in egg white and coat with dry ingredients. 8 Fry in hot oil until golden brown. **sauce:** 1 Combine all ingredients for the dip. 2 Serve *adobong moderno* with *adobo* dip.

chili crab

1 Wash the crab, break off the claws and chop the rest of the body into pieces. Drain off the water and set aside. **2** In a large wok, fry the dried shrimp, ginger, red chili, garlic and onion. **3** Add chili sauce, tomato sauce, sugar, $^1/_2$ tsp of salt, soya sauce and the chicken stock. **4** When the stock is boiling. Add the crab that was set aside. **5** Cover with a lid and simmer over high heat for 5 to 7 minutes till shells turn a bright red. **6** Turn heat off, and then add the mixture of corn flour and water. **7** Add the egg and spread it around evenly. **8** Garnish with coriander leaf before serving.

singapore

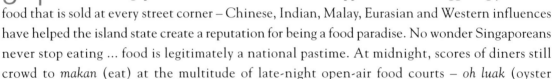

Singapore's multi-cultural mix is most apparent in the staggering jumble of food that is sold at every street corner – Chinese, Indian, Malay, Eurasian and Western influences have helped the island state create a reputation for being a food paradise. No wonder Singaporeans never stop eating ... food is legitimately a national pastime. At midnight, scores of diners still crowd to *makan* (eat) at the multitude of late-night open-air food courts – *oh luak* (oyster omelette), *chai tow kway* (fried carrot cake) and Teochew porridge are hot favourites.

Immigrants from China, India, Indonesia, the Malayan Straits and many other countries brought with them their favourite dishes – leading to the dazzling array of dishes available. The cultural cuisines however have remained largely distinct. From the Chinese, Hainanese chicken rice (steamed chicken and rice) is perhaps the most popular, while the Indians boast the breakfast favourite – the tossed Indian bread called *prata* – lusciously dipped in spicy south Indian curry. Malay favourites like *nasi goreng* – fried rice with egg, chicken and *achar* (pickles) – are also staples.

There is one exceptional local fusion, however – the *Nonya* cuisine. This is food of the *Peranakans*, a people whose heritage stems from intermarriage between the early Chinese settlers and the local Malays as far back as the 15th century. *Nonya* cuisine is a unique combination of the two cultures, using Chinese ingredients – pork, vegetables and seasonings – and blending them with Malay spices and herbs. *Buah keluak* (chicken braised with an indigenous nut in a rich dark sauce), *itek tim* (duck soup with salted vegetables), and *otak-otak* (banana leaf-wrapped fish paste) reflect this unique duality. One must not forget *belacan* (chili shrimp paste) that is omnipresent at every meal.

Above all, the complexities of *Nonya* food – and in no small part, its laborious preparation methods – give an indication of the multi-layered texture of food in Singapore. And that nothing is too much trouble for the satiation of a demanding appetite.

1½ kg crab
50 g dried shrimp
20 g ginger
150 g red chili, chopped
30 g garlic, minced
30 g onion, minced
100 g chili sauce
80 g tomato sauce
1 tbsp sugar
½ tsp salt
½ tbsp soya sauce
4 cups chicken stock
1 egg
½ tsp corn flour,
   mixed with ¼ cup of water
1 stem coriander leaf

thailand

Some say Thai food is the tastiest of all Asian food and it is hard to argue with that. Seasoning is the magic word when it comes to a true Thai meal. Widely known for being hot and spicy, almost all Thai food include basic ingredients such as garlic, chilies, lime juice, lemon grass, fresh coriander leaf and *nam pla* (fermented fish sauce) or *kapi* (shrimp paste).

Since rice is a staple, it is usually eaten at every meal with soups, curries, fried vegetables and *nam phrik*, a hot sauce prepared in a variety of ways which differ from region to region. In general, the basic ingredients of *nam phrik* include shrimp paste, garlic, chili, fermented fish sauce and lemon juice. The common seasonings in Thai food include *galangal*, black pepper, ground peanut, tamarind juice, ginger and coconut milk. As a result, it takes hours to prepare a proper Thai meal in the traditional way – a process that involves much peeling, chopping and pounding. Visitors are often surprised, too, that insects factor in traditional meals – crickets, silkworm larvae and red ant larvae are some common delicacies.

From region to region, basic characteristics differ. In the central region, food is hot, salty, sweet and sour. Rice is served with different types of *nam phrik* and soups such as *tom yam kung* (prawn soup with lemon grass). Dishes usually contain a lot of condiments and spices. In the North, food is mild or hot, salty and sour, but never sweet. Sticky rice is served with boiled vegetables, *nam phrik oong* (*nam phrik* with minced pork, tomato and chili sauce) and soups or curries. In the Northeast, favourite foods include *som tam* (papaya salad), and *larp* (sour minced meat salad). And in the South, curries are popular and prepared with lots of spices and condiments. The best and most popular Thai dish has to be the exotic *tom yam kung*, a uniquely piquant prawn soup that is renowned for its simplicity, creativity, artistic flair and delicious taste. It is perhaps the epitome of unforgettable Thai cuisine.

tom yam kung (spicy and sour prawn soup)

1 Pour the water into a saucepan. Bring to a boil. **2** Add the lemongrass and kaffir lime leaves, then the prawns. Cover and simmer for three minutes. **3** Add the mushrooms, salt and pepper. Simmer for a few more minutes. **4** Remove from the heat and season with fish sauce, lime juice and chili powder. **5** Sprinkle with chopped coriander leaves. **6** Serves about 4.

10 king prawns, shelled
1 cup mushrooms
1 stalk lemongrass, chopped
2 kaffir lime leaves
½ tsp salt
½ tsp ground pepper
2 tbsp fish sauce
2 tbsp lime juice
½ tsp chili powder
1 tbsp coriander leaves, chopped
1 pint water

vietnam

vietnam is a land of beautiful geography – unspoiled coastline, sheltered harbours, fertile lowlands and vast forests. With this varied terrain, it has become a major supplier of rice, fish, fresh fruit and vegetables to Southeast Asia. The Mekong River, one of Southeast Asia's longest, is a treasure trove of seafood, an integral part of the Vietnamese diet. What is deemed as Vietnamese cuisine varies depending on the region. For example, the food from the cooler North uses stewing as a common method, not too different from that found across the nearby Chinese border. Two famous northern Vietnamese dishes are *phó* (a tasty beef broth with rice noodles and fresh herbs) and *bun cha* (an aromatic dish of barbecued pork eaten in broth with noodles and herbs). In the central heartland, dining has developed into an art form. Small portions in multiple courses give common fare an air of sophistication. Signature dishes of central Vietnam include *banh khoai* (a delicious eggy pancake), *banh bo hue* (a soup and noodle dish) and the ever-popular *cha gio* (spring rolls) and *chao tom* (sugar cane shrimps). In the temperate South, the food bears close resemblance to that of Cambodia, Thailand and Malaysia, as it is varied and is generously spiced with fresh chilies, coconut milk, herbs and spices. One common ingredient throughout Vietnam is the ubiquitous *nuoc mam*, a pungent, salty pale brown fermented fish sauce, which is used in marinades, sauces, salad dressing and cooking.

Vietnamese cookery may generally be described as textural and tangy. It is also highly fragrant because of the pervasive use of fresh leaves and herbs. Light and refreshing, true Vietnamese cuisine offers a delightful treat for one's eyes and palate.

3 onions
1 tbsp peanut oil
2½ kg beef and chicken bones
4 slices ginger, julienned
2 carrots, julienned
1 cinnamon stick
1 star anise
2 cloves, whole
1 tsp black peppercorns, whole
2 cloves garlic, smashed
250 g fresh bean sprouts
250 g beef sirloin, sliced very thinly
   across the grain
1 scallion, finely sliced
¼ cup fresh cilantro or coriander
   leaves, chopped
4 serrano chilies, sliced
2 limes, cut into wedges
rice sticks/noodles, soaked in
   hot water for 30 minutes, drained
3 tbsp fish sauce
fresh black pepper to taste

banh phó bo (beef noodle soup)

1 Slice 2 of the onions into ²/₃-cm slices. 2 Heat 1 tbsp oil in a frying pan and cook the onion, stirring, until slightly brown. Remove and drain. 3 Slice the remaining onion into paper-thin slices and set aside. 4 Rinse bones and set in a stockpot. Cover with cold water and then bring slowly to a boil. Reduce heat and simmer uncovered. Skim off foam. 5 After 15 minutes, add browned onion and ginger, carrots, cinnamon, star anise, cloves, garlic and peppercorns. Bring to a boil. Simmer partially covered for up to 12 hours, skimming the foam off regularly. If necessary, add more water to the bones to ensure that they are completely covered. 6 Strain the stock, skim and discard any fat. 7 When it's time to serve, arrange sliced beef on a platter. Garnish with reserved sliced onions and scallion. 8 On another platter, arrange the fresh bean sprouts, coriander leaves or cilantro, chilies and lime wedges. 9 Plunge the rice sticks into boiling water to heat. Drain and place equal portions in each serving soup bowl. 10 Heat the stock to boiling, season with fish sauce and pepper. Pour into soup bowls over the rice sticks and serve. 11 Diners add the sliced beef and garnish into the bowl, as desired, and stir to cook briefly.

THE PRINCIPLES OF AYURVEDA

The basis of *Ayurveda* is the one factor that unifies all the diverse elements of Indian cuisine. It provides the philosophical underpinning of an Indian meal.

Ayurveda is more than just a system of medicine. It focuses on harmony between the mind, body and soul, and is thus a total system for balanced living. Here, the ultimate role of food is to create equilibrium among the three primary *Ayurvedic* life forces – *vata* or air, *pita* or fire, *kapha* or phlegm – present in each individual. Food helps bring these life forces in tune with a person's *Ayurvedic* mental type – *satvic* or pure, *rajasvic* or material, and *tamasvic* or gross.

In the *Ayurvedic* tradition, what we eat balance the proportions of the body elements (seven in total according to *Ayurveda*) and ensures proper flow through the various channels that nourish them. Various foods are classified on the basis of their *rasas* or flavours and their effect on the body – cooling, astringent, heating, purifying and so on. For example, dates and figs are both sweet, and have heating propensities. But figs also have purgative and purifying qualities. Spices and herbs have medicinal properties assigned to them in the *Ayurvedic* tradition, yet that have been confirmed by modern science, for example the antiseptic qualities of turmeric, circulatory benefits of garlic and the anti-bacterial effect of curry leaves.

dhoklas (steamed savoury cakes from gujarat)

In Gujarat, the predominance of Jainism has influenced the preference for vegetarianism. *Dhoklas* are often eaten as a snack or a part of a meal, with accompanying mango puree or tamarind *chutney*.

1 Wash *chana dhal*, rice and *urad dhal* in water. Cover with water by 3 inches and soak for 8 hours. Drain. **2** Blend mixture in a food processor or blender. When it becomes a coarse paste, add 1 cup of water in a gentle and steady stream. Continue to blend for 6 – 8 minutes till it turns an airy batter. **3** Empty batter into a bowl, cover with a plate and leave for about 24 hours or until the batter is filled with bubbles. **4** Put salt, ginger, green chilies and cumin seeds into the bowl with the batter but do not stir in yet. **5** Prepare utensils for steaming. **6** Combine ¼ cup vegetable oil with ¼ cup water and bring to a boil. Take it off the flame and stir in bicarbonate of soda. Add this mixture into the batter and stir to mix everything. **7** Pour batter into a tin container or deep-dished plate and set in steamer. Cover and steam for about 20 minutes or till a toothpick inserted into the centre comes out clean. **8** Remove from steamer, cool for 10 – 15 minutes, then cut into 2.5-cm cubes and arrange on serving platter. **9** For the *baghar*, heat 3 tablespoons of oil in a frying pan. When oil becomes very hot, add mustard seeds and sesame seeds. When seeds start to pop, add whole red chilies, stir, and when they darken, pour the seasoned oil, with the spices, over the *dokhla* cubes. **10** Garnish with fresh coriander and coconut before serving at warm or room temperature. **11** Serves 6 – 8.

india

Despite the omnipresence of Indian restaurants around the world, the concept of Indian cuisine is mired in what is called *Moghlai* cuisine – complicated dishes with rich, heavy sauces such as butter chicken or *rogan josh* (a lamb curry). In fact, Indian cuisine consists of a vast spectrum that varies not only from region to region but also from community to community, based on such things as geographical locations, religious traditions and differing income levels. For example, in Kerala, there are distinct variations in food eaten by indigenous Namboodri Brahmins, Syrian Christians and Malabar Muslims; and Udipi food is clearly different from the food of the Coorg, though both regions are in the same state of Karnataka.

For the most part, regional differences define the variety of dishes in India. Fish is a fixture on the Bengali table and as one moves West, meat becomes more of a factor in the diet. Vegetarianism reins in Gujarat where the desert-like geography promotes staples like grain and pulses. And in the northern reaches of Kashmir, meats – grilled or in curries – are the courses of choice.

Indian cooking has also been touched by foreign influences. Virtually every cooking technique existing in the world has a parallel in some part of India. However, there are also unique Indian variations such as the *tandoor*, a Punjabi clay oven, or the *dum* style of cooking where all ingredients are put in a claypot, sealed with dough, buried in hot coals and left to cook overnight.

Indian cuisine generally finds expression in the use of a medley of seasonings. Spices are often used in various combinations to create variations on the six basic *rasas* or flavours in the *Ayurvedic* (see insert) tradition – sour, salty, sweet, bitter, pungent and astringent.

Though often associated with its richness, an Indian meal is actually a good example of 'balance', at least in the Western sense. The focus is on carbohydrates (bread from whole-wheat flour or corn in the North, rice in the South) eaten with a variety of suitable accompaniments. The latter might include several vegetables, meat, and yoghurt, and ending with fresh fruit.

Even in its presentation, the typical Indian meal exemplifies the concept of equilibrium. Food is often placed in a *thali* (or plate) where the carbohydrate takes centre stage surrounded by individual bowls or mounds of accompanying items, revealing a range of colours, textures and aromas – a feast for the body, mind and soul.

180 g skinned *channa dal*
(a kind of yellow split pea)
75 g long-grained rice
35 g skinned *urad dal*
1 tsp salt
1¼ tsp ginger, peeled
and finely grated
1 tsp fresh green chilies,
finely minced
¼ tsp whole cumin seeds
¼ cup vegetable oil
¼ tsp bicarbonate of soda
water

garnish
4 tbsp fresh green corander,
chopped
2 – 3 tbsp grated fresh
coconut

baghar
3 tbsp vegetable oil
1 tbsp whole black
mustard seeds
2 tbsp whole sesame seeds
2 – 3 whole dried red chilies

kozhi varatha kosambu (chicken chettinad from tamil nadu)

The strong Southeast Asian influence in the cuisine from this region probably came from the trade between the two areas over the last thousand years. Star anise, for one, is native to China and the chicken here is cut into small pieces on the bone, a typical Chinese trait. This dish is drier than a normal curry, so it is traditionally eaten with lemon or tomato flavoured rice. It also goes well with North Indian breads like *naan*, *paratha* or *poori*.

1 Rub chicken with salt and turmeric powder, set aside for 5 minutes, then stir-fry in oil seasoned by the *baghar* or *tarka* technique. **2** The *baghar* or *tarka* technique requires the oil to be seasoned before it is used for stir-frying. **3** First, heat the oil on a medium-high flame. When hot, put in mustard seeds. When the seeds start popping, add *urad dhal*. As the *dhal* turns red, add the fennel seeds and the whole red chilies. **4** When the chilies darken, add the onions and sauté till light brown. **5** Add the chicken pieces and stir-fry for about 10 – 13 minutes, sprinkling salted water (use ¼ tsp salt in 3 tbsp water) from time to time till cooked.

1¼ to 1½ kg chicken pieces on the
    bone, or chicken drumsticks
1 tsp salt
¼ tsp turmeric powder
1 tsp fennel seeds
1 onion, chopped
1 5-cm long cinnamon stick
3 green cardamoms
2 cloves
¾ tsp *garam masala* powder
½ cup of oil
½ fresh coconut
½ star anise
2 tsp fresh ginger, finely chopped
2 tsp garlic, finely chopped
3 medium tomatoes, chopped
juice of ½ lime
a few curry leaves
salt to taste
½ cup coriander leaves, chopped,
    for garnish

baghar
½ tsp skinned *urad dal*
    (small, black-skinned oval beans
    often used for lentil curries in
    North India)
½ tsp black mustard seeds
5 whole dried red chilies
1 tsp fennel seeds

macher jhol (fish in mustard gravy from west bengal)

spiced water

600 g fish, cut into pieces
2 tbsp poppy seeds
2 tbsp brown mustard seeds
1 tsp turmeric powder
2 2-cm piece fresh ginger
6 garlic cloves (optional)
2 – 3 green chilies
1 onion, coarsely chopped
2 tsp coriander powder
2 tsp cumin powder
½ – 1½ tsp red chili powder
4 tbsp oil, preferably mustard oil
3 tomatoes, pureed (optional)
juice of ½ lime (optional)
a few curry leaves or coriander
leaves for garnish salt

baghar (optional)

¼ tsp nigella seeds
4 whole dried red chilies
2 bay leaves

It is a rare Bengali who does not passionately adore fish. *Macher jhol* simply means fish in 'spiced water' or gravy. This is a standard dish in every Bengali home and is traditionally eaten – head, skin, bones and all – with boiled rice.

1 Wash fish thoroughly. Smear with salt and turmeric mixed together (about ½ tsp each), leave for ½ hour. **2** Toast poppy seeds for 2 minutes on a griddle on low heat. Soak in a little water for 15 minutes, and pound in a mortar and pestle. **3** Grind together the poppy seeds, mustard seeds, turmeric, ginger, garlic, green chilies, onion, coriander, cumin, red chili powder and 1¼ tsp salt, along with ½ cup water, to make a paste. **4** In a large frying pan, heat oil over moderate heat. If a *baghar* is used, add the black mustard seeds, dried red chilies and bay leaves to season the oil. **5** Add the spice paste and fry for 6 – 7 minutes, stirring continuously, sprinkling a little water once in a while to keep paste from drying out (up to ½ cup of water). **6** If using tomatoes, add them now, then sauté for 5 minutes adding 2 to 3 tbsp water if required. **7** Pour in 2 cups water and the lime juice, simmer for 5 minutes on low heat. Salt to taste. **8** Add fish pieces and cook on medium heat for 2 minutes, spooning sauce over the fish. Then cover and simmer for 10 – 15 minutes till done. **9** Sprinkle with fresh coriander or curry leaves before serving. **10** Serves about 4.

red kidney bean and turnip stew
(from kashmir)

1 cup red kidney beans,
picked over, washed and
soaked overnight
4 medium-sized turnips,
peeled and quartered
¼ tsp powdered ginger
¼ tsp turmeric powder
1 tsp salt
½ tsp red chili powder
4 tbsp vegetable oil
1 medium onion, halved
length-wise and finely
sliced into half rings
2 – 3 garlic cloves,
peeled and finely chopped

Kashmir is a region that produces exotic dishes from indigenous products such as the morel, dried red cockscomb flowers and saffron. Both the Muslims and Hindus of Kashmir eat a lot of meat and share many of the same recipes. Muslims, however, tend to use more garlic and onions while Hindus prefer *asafetida*, a strong-smelling resin whose aroma is likened to truffles.

The following dish is generally eaten in the biting cold of the Kashmiri winter.

1 Boil kidney beans in 5 cups of water for about 10 minutes, then leave to simmer. **2** Mix ginger, turmeric, salt and chili powder with 1 tbsp water into a smooth paste. **3** Heat oil over medium heat. When hot, fry turnip pieces till brown on all sides. Remove. **4** Fry onion in the same oil till golden brown. Turn the heat down slightly and fry garlic for a few seconds. **5** Put in the spice paste prepared earlier, stir once and take pan off the heat. **6** After the beans have been simmering for 45 minutes, add the turnips and the spice/onion mixture to it. **7** Bring the beans to a vigorous simmer, then turn the heat down to low, cover partially and simmer until cooked thoroughly, about another 45 minutes. **8** Serves 6.

jhinka masala (shrimp curry)

1 Marinate shrimp with salt and turmeric. Set aside for about 15 minutes. **2** Combine mustard, cumin, garlic, ginger, chillies and lemon juice in a blender and puree. Set aside. **3** Heat oil in a skillet over medium-high heat. Cook onions until soft. Add pureed spice mixture. Cook for about 5 minutes till fragrant. **4** Stir in tomato and cook until soft. Add shrimps, stirring gently. **5** Pour in the water and bring to a boil, stirring constantly. Reduce heat to medium, cover, and cook until shrimp are just opaque, about 5 minutes. **6** Serve with basmati rice.

bangladesh

The region of Bengal has historically been one of great influence to the Indian sub-continent. Even after the 1971 War of Liberation, which resulted in the creation of an independent Bangladesh, Bengalese art, culture and food maintained their relevance in South Asia.

The nickname 'bheto Bengali', or 'rice-eating Bengali', distinguishes the people's affinity to the sacred grain. Rice, easily cultivated within Bangladesh's well irrigated landscape, forms the basis of most meals. Curries are popularly eaten as an apt accompaniment. The Bangladeshi version tends to have thinner gravies compared to their counterpart in India. Bangladeshi food is simple and nutritious. *Khichuri*, a lentil stew made of dhal, features commonly in a cook's repertoire. Other everyday foods might include *bhaji*, a stir-fry of vegetables, or *bhorta*, a soft mash made of cooked vegetables or fish. Needless to say, these are almost always eaten with rice.

Desserts may be divided into two main groups. The milk-based variety includes *chhana bhora*, which are cottage cheese dumplings soaked in syrup. Otherwise, rice pudding desserts offer an alternative. These may be made with gourd, or *halva* – dough made from eggs, butter, sugar, milk and carrot. Another popular dessert, *pati shapta pitha* is a mat-like pancake prepared with a myriad of fillings. Bangladesh is a land blessed with rivers, lakes and a long coastline abutting the Bay of Bengal. As such, fish and seafood are also a main part of the indigenous diet. Even though the country is predominantly Muslim, the level of religious tolerance is impressive. Christians, Buddhists, Hindus and Muslims celebrate their major annual festivals and national holidays, all in a grand display of gastronomic tolerance.

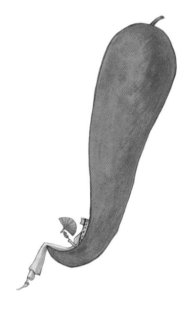

500 g medium-size shrimps, peeled, de-veined
2 cups of water
½ tsp salt
¼ tsp turmeric
½ tsp mustard seeds
1 tsp cumin seeds
4 garlic cloves, peeled
1 2-cm piece fresh ginger, peeled
2 dried red chillies, stemmed, and de-seeded
1 tbsp lemon juice
2 tbsp mustard oil
1 cup onions, chopped
1½ cups tomato, chopped
freshly cooked basmati rice

bhutan & nepal

In the high altitudes of Bhutan and Nepal, food as sustenance is a main concern. And despite the inevitable influences from nearby India and China, dishes at the roof of the world are predominantly created from providence and the need to withstand the inevitable long cold winters.

If there's one thing the Bhutanese cannot do without it is their beloved chilies. In fact, their cuisine is predominantly characterised by the bi-lateral partnership of chili and cheese (similar to cottage cheese). *Ema datsi* (chili and cheese) has come to earn national status, slowly evolving into many forms: *kewa datsi* (potato and cheese); *shamu datsi* (mushroom and cheese); and *nake datsi* (fiddlehead fern and cheese) to name a few. Occasionally, a meat dish like *pak sha pa*, streaky pork with the skin on, breaks the chili/cheese stronghold. This is unanimously eaten with rice and possibly an accompaniment of *azay* (crushed red chili with tamarind).

The Bhutanese cuisine derives much of its food and vegetables from nature. In the higher altitudes, the largely nomadic communities have a rich diet of dairy products. A red variety of mountain rice is eaten in the western part of the country, buckwheat is a staple in the central valley of Bumthang, and maize is the mainstay in the East. *Suja* or butter tea is the libation of choice, made by churning butter with a brick tea resulting in a strong, distinctive brew.

Both Bhutan and Nepal share some common dishes, like the Tibetan-style *momos* (dumplings filled with cheese or pork), and *thukpa* (noodles). But this is pretty much where the similarity ends. Despite its juxtaposition between two culinary giants – India and China – food in Nepal is simple at best. Rice is a given, and this is usually supplemented by dhal (lentils) and vegetables cooked with ginger, garlic, or chili. *Achar* made from pickled radishes have an Indian disposition, so do *chapattis* (wheat flat bread) eaten with curries. The Nepalese do have a sweet tooth and are somewhat partial to sweet and spicy snacks like *jelebis* and *laddus*.

dough
3 cups all-purpose flour
1 cup water

meat filling
500 g ground beef, extra lean
1 onion, chopped
250 g daikon, spinach
  or cabbage, chopped fine
1 garlic clove, minced
1 tsp fresh ginger, grated
2 green onions, chopped
2 tbsp fresh cilantro, chopped
salt to taste
chili sauce or soy sauce

momos (steamed dumplings)

1 Mix flour and water; knead and form into a ball. Let rise, covered with a wet towel for half an hour. **2** Bring a large pot of water to boil. Cut dough into 12 – 18 pieces and roll into small flat circles. **3** Mash all filling ingredients. Place a spoonful of filling on each dough circle, folding over and crimping to seal. **4** Place dumplings in a steamer and steam on high for about half an hour. **5** Serve with chili sauce or soy sauce.

indian sub-continent

afghanistan.pakistan.maldives.sri lanka The Indian sub-continent is the birthplace of some of the world's oldest civilisations. And over the centuries, food in this region has been greatly influenced by surrounding cultures and past colonial heritage. The cuisine of Pakistan and Afghanistan reflect the influence from India, Arabia and Persia, while the food of Sri Lanka is a conglomeration of Dutch, Portuguese, British, Malay, Arab and South Indian.

Rice, fish (mainly tuna and sailfish) and coconut form the core of the Maldives staple. Fish is served at virtually every meal, including breakfast. The national dish here is *garudiya*, a fish soup made from a pungent treacle-like fish stock, and is accompanied by rice, lime, onions and green chili. Some favourite *hedhikaa* (snacks) include *gulha* (fried fish balls with an outer coating of rice or flour), *kulhi boa kiba* (spicy fish cake with garlic and chili) and *bajiya* (samosa-shaped pastry stuffed with onions, fish and coconut). The fruit of the screw pine makes for an interesting dessert when mixed with bananas, sugar and grated coconut, together with *raa* (Maldivian toddy), a sweet and delicious drink.

The national food in Sri Lanka is rice and curry and their many variants. The curries range from non-spicy creamy white, to brown (using raw curry powder), to bright red (using fiery hot pounded red chilies) and even a black version, which tastes a lot better than it looks. Their curry and rice meal is completed by *mallung* (shredded green vegetables and dried shrimps mixed with grated coconut and spices), *papadams* (crispy fried wafers), pickles and *chutneys*. A traditional favourite dessert is thick buffalo curd (yoghurt) topped with syrup from the *kitul* or coconut palm, accompanied by *thambili* (juice of the king coconut either taken plain or flavoured with sugar, lime and a pinch of salt).

Pakistan's signature dishes include *haleem* (pieces of meat cooked in a smooth sauce made from grains) and *nihari* (large chunks of beef, brain, tongue and marrow added to a highly seasoned gravy), served with slivers of ginger, onions, fresh chilies, chopped coriander, limejuice and *naan*. The country is also famous for *tandoori* chicken – a quartered chicken steeped in marinade and barbecued in an underground clay oven or *tandoor*. The perfect accompaniment to this would be *lassi* (a savoury, sweetened or fruit-flavoured yoghurt-drink), or *nimbu pani* (freshly squeezed lime juice).

An integral ingredient in Afghan food is *maust* (yoghurt, frequently drained to make a thick cream cheese-like *chakah*). Typical Afghan rice dishes like *chalau* and *palau* are similar to the Iranian and Pakistani-Indian rice dishes. Afghans generally like their food a little on the oily side, either from lamb fat, vegetable oil or *ghee*. At any given meal, one will always find rice served with the standard vegetables, salad, pickles, yoghurt and bread, accompanied by *dug* (yoghurt drink) or *murgh* (buttermilk), followed by typical desserts of saffron threads, unsalted pistachio nuts, almonds and walnuts.

masbaiy

1 Fry the onions, garlic, curry leaves and *rampe* leaves in *ghee* until onions turn brown. 2 Add in the cloves, cardamoms, cinnamon, and tuna and mix well. 3 Add the rice and fry lightly. 4 Add the coconut milk, water, turmeric, cherry peppers, black peppercorns and salt to taste. Stir once and bring to a boil. Reduce heat, and cover the pot. 5 Simmer till the water is evaporated and rice is fluffy. Remove from heat and let sit for 10 minutes. Stir the rice to separate the grains. 6 Serves about 4.

450 g *patna* rice
   (excess starch washed off)
300 g tuna
   (fresh, cut into cubes)
6 large onions, thinly sliced
4 garlic cloves, sliced
7 cherry peppers
1 tsp black peppercorns
2 cinnamon sticks
4 cloves
7 cardamoms
½ tsp turmeric powder
2 curry leaves
12 *rampe* leaves
100 g *ghee* (clarified butter)
1 litre coconut milk
1½ litre water
salt to taste

kiri bath (milk rice)

500 g raw rice
1 large coconut,
   shredded
10 – 12 cups of water
3 tsp salt
3 – 4 cardamoms,
   crushed

This is the national dish of Sri Lanka and occupies a vital position in all auspicious events like weddings, house-warming ceremonies, as well as in Buddhist and Hindu cultural functions.

1 Wash and drain rice. Set aside. 2 Mix about 3 cups of water with the coconut. Squeeze the coconut in the water until all the juice is extracted. Drain this coconut mixture and set the liquid aside. This is the first extract. 3 Pour another 2 cups of water into the coconut. Repeat the same and squeeze the liquid out to a separate bowl. This is the second extract. 4 Repeat to obtain the 3rd extract. Set aside separately. 5 Place washed rice in a large pot. Add the 2nd and 3rd extract of coconut milk with salt and crushed cardamoms. Heat the pot till the liquid boils lightly. Lower the heat and simmer covered. 6 When the coconut milk level is simmered down to the same level as the rice, add the first extract of coconut milk. Stir well and cook until the mixture is a thick mass. 7 Makes 6 – 8 portions.

raita

1 Whip the yogurt with the milk. 2 Add the rest of the ingredients and whip again. 3 Add the cucumber and garnish with cumin powder. Serve chilled.

2 cups yogurt,
   whipped (add ¼ cup
   milk if a lighter
   consistency is
   required)
½ cucumber, chopped
2 tbsp sugar
½ tsp cumin powder
¼ tsp black pepper
   (optional)
salt to taste

central
pacific

3

4

6

5   2

11

9

7

8

12

10

1

central pacific islands

kiribati.marshall islands.micronesia.nauru.palau.solomon islands.tonga.tuvalu and vanuatu

All along the Central Pacific Ocean, the islands of Kiribati, Marshall Islands, Tonga, Solomon Islands, Vanuatu, Micronesia, Nauru, Palau, and Tuvalu, form a necklace of crystal waters and immaculate beaches. The people here live mostly in an agrarian society, with their livelihood dependent primarily on farming. The staple foods among the different islands are quite alike and are pretty much based on fish, taro, sweet potato, coconut and yam that are grown in all of the islands. However, although the basic ingredients may be the same, how these are used vary with the different islands. They also share a love for *kava*, a potent narcotic drink that relaxes the mind and body and leaves no hangover the next day.

Food in Vanuatu is quite basic, but the few common dishes can manifest in several ways or forms. The national dish is *laplap*, a bland paste of ground manioc, taro or yam with wild spinach and grated coconut. To this base, pork, beef, poultry, seafood or, sometimes, even flying fox is added, and the paste is wrapped in banana leaves and baked in an *umu* (ground oven). For vegetarians, there is *nalot*, a delicious mixture of taro, banana or breadfruit mixed with grated coconut and water. The *kava* served in Vanuatu is legendary, being much more potent than that served in other Pacific islands.

The traditional Tongan feast is a treat for the palate. It is cooked in the *umu*, and usually comprises root vegetables like taro and sweet potato, coconut, fresh fruit, roasted suckling pig, corned beef, fish and shellfish. Preferred beverages to accompany the meal include *kava*, fresh coconut juice, locally grown Royal Coffee and beer.

The food of a country or region is often seen as a reflection of the lifestyle of its inhabitants. If that was the case, Central Pacific cuisines speak volumes about the hospitable, honest and humble character of its people.

fiji.papua new guinea.samoa The island nations of Samoa, Fiji and Papua New Guinea are essentially separate countries, but bear some similarity with each other. Their people generally live off the land and sea for their daily sustenance, creating delicious concoctions with what they have.

In Samoa, food is derived mainly from tropical crops, root vegetables, coconut products, fresh fruit, pork, chicken and seafood. Like most of the islands in the Central Pacific, the meal is usually cooked in an *umu*, an underground oven. Samoans are fond of *taofolo* (kneaded breadfruit and sweet coconut cream wrapped in taro leaves and baked), *pisupo* (canned corned beef and young taro wrapped in a breadfruit leaf and baked on hot stones) and *fa'ausi* (a pudding made of grated taro and coconut cream). There is a wide usage of coconut cream in their recipes, as in *suafa'i* (ripe bananas with coconut cream), *faia'i'fe'e* or *faiaipusi* (octopus or sea eel in coconut cream). The national drink is *kava*, a beverage made from the ground roots of pepper plants, which has a mild tranquilising effect.

On the same token, the Fijian diet also involves a healthy smattering of fish, seafood and ground crops. Their national favourites include *ika* (baked fish in coconut cream with tapioca, taro, breadfruit and sweet potato); *duruka* (young sugar cane) or *vakalolo* (fish and prawns), both baked in *lolo*; and *kokoda* (diced raw fish marinated in coconut cream and lime juice). To accompany their meals, the Fijians are partial to their own local bitter beer, brandy, gin, vodka and rum. In addition, Fijians also enjoy Indian cuisine, like curries with *dhal* (lentil soup), *roti* (a flat *tortilla*-like bread), and *samosas* (potato and vegetable wrapped in dough and deep-fried) with their *lassi* (a drink comprising yoghurt and water).

Papua New Guinea is fast becoming a major seafood producer in the region. It naturally follows that seafood is one of the major dietary items among the natives. Although, generally speaking, the staples of Papua New Guineans are simple – starchy versions of carbohydrates, great seafood is available all along the coast. *Saksak* (sago) is commonly found in the low-lying region, whereas it is sweet potato that is eaten widely in the highlands.

This is one part of the globe still untouched by commercialism. And the wealth of fresh seafood and succulent agricultural products is virtually unknown, and unmatched, by the rest of the world.

125 g butter or margarine
½ cup sugar
2 eggs
1½ cups self-raising flour, sifted
2 tbsp cornflour
½ cup milk
1 tbsp instant coffee powder
1 tsp hot water
2 tbsp cocoa, sifted

icing
1½ cup sugar
1 tbsp cocoa
2 tsp instant coffee powder
2 tbsp milk
2 tsp melted butter or margarine

mocha loaf

Coffee is the major export crop of Papua New Guinea. Although almost all of the coffee beans grown here are exported in their raw form, there has been a push to process the product locally. The following recipe is just one of the many local ways in which coffee is used.

cake: 1 Mix butter and sugar until light and creamy. Add beaten eggs one at a time, beating well after each addition. **2** Fold in sifted flour alternating with milk. Divide mixture in half. **3** To one half, add the sifted cocoa, mix well. **4** To the other half add the coffee powder, dissolve with the hot water and mix thoroughly. **5** Spoon coffee mixture into a greased loaf tin. Bake in an oven on moderate heat for 50 – 60 minutes or until a cake tester comes out clean. **6** Turn out on a rack and cool. **icing: 1** Stir icing sugar, cocoa and coffee powder into a bowl. **2** Add the milk and butter and beat until smooth. **3** Top the cake with the icing.

corn soup

1 If fresh corn is used, strip the kernels off the cob. Set kernels aside. **2** Melt butter in a large saucepan and gently fry the onions, garlic and cumin seeds. **3** Add the stock and bring to a boil. Then add the potatoes and simmer for 10 minutes. **4** Add the corn and parsley and simmer for another 15 minutes. **5** Stir in the cheese and season with salt and pepper. Add a little cream to thicken and serve as soon as the cheese has melted into the soup. **6** Garnish with chopped chives and parsley before serving.

1 tbsp butter
2 onions, chopped
1 clove garlic, chopped
2 tsp cumin seeds
1 litre chicken stock
3 potatoes, peeled and cubed
3 cups corn kernels
  (fresh or frozen)
1 handful parsley, chopped
salt and pepper to taste
1 cup cheese, grated
cream to thicken

garnish
chives and parsley, chopped

australiasia

1

2

WHAT YOU HEAR ISN'T WHAT YOU GET

English might be the *lingua franca* in Australia, but quite often you are left scratching your head when you hear an Aussie shoot the breeze about his favourite foods. The following is a sample of the colourful slangs popular in the land down under.

bikkies biscuits
bottle shop liquor shop
chiko roll australian junk food
chook chicken
cut lunch sandwiches
damper a loaf made of flour and water
dead horse tomato sauce
fairy floss candy floss
grog general term for beer
icy-pole ice popsicle or ice cream on a stick
lolly water soft drink
milko milkman
sherbet another name for beer
snag sausage
stubby small bottle of beer
tucker food

lobster and mango salad with basil vinaigrette

This dish sparked an eclectic wave that has since swept the nation. The simplicity of blending fresh seafood with tropical fruits evokes a marriage based on fundamental values. Some relationships are just meant to be.

1 Combine all court bouillon ingredients in a pot and boil. **2** Add lobster tails and simmer until the shell turns red. **3** Remove lobster from the pot and let cool. **4** Remove meat from the lobster tail and cut into 1-cm thickness. **sauce: 5** Blend the vinegar, oil, garlic and basil leaves in a food processor until smooth. **6** Add salt and pepper to taste. **7** Serve lobster with sauce and sliced mangoes arranged on a plate as shown.

australia

From a food point of view, Australia is the closest one can come to a prototypical example of how different worlds can come together to affect change. Over two and a half centuries after Britain disposed of its unwanted citizenry on this island-country-continent, the demographical and gastronomical transformations evident point to a future of multi-cultural proportions.

For the most part, typical Australian food has always hung onto the apron strings of its British heritage. The innocuous meat pie and lamington (not a small furry animal, but a kind of cake) used to make up the Australian national cuisine, and the country used to be ranked as the highest per capita tea consumers in the world. But things change. From the 1950s, immigrants from Greece, Italy, Lebanon and other Mediterranean countries brought along their colourful cuisines to their new home. The Vietnamese diaspora brought an Asian element and the subsequent migrants from Southeast Asia opened the country to multi-layers of cooking ingredients and methods. What these different food approaches have done is combine the abundant fresh produce and livestock in this Southern Hemisphere land of plenty with classical – Eastern and Western – cooking methods. The result is a 'pan-Australasian' cuisine that is as fresh and bold as the country appeared to Captain James Cook when he took his 'Endeavour' into the shelter of Botany Bay in 1770.

The bounties of Australia have grown exponentially over the decades. Australia is now known as a hotbed of agricultural products, livestock and seafood. Fruits from Queensland, salmon, oysters and rock lobster off the coast of Tasmania, cheeses of Gippsland in Victoria, and wheat and cattle in virtually every state are just some items on the country's vast menu. Australia's indigenous food stock is also coming into its own. Game like the iconic kangaroo, and fruits like the *quandong* (a South Australian native peach) are standing up to claim their culinary birthright. And all across the Barossa Valley of South Australia, Hunter Valley of New South Wales, and Swan Valley of Perth, Australian wines are raising vintners' eyebrows around the world.

Today, the Australian attitude towards food is a simple case of cultural mix and match. *Burramandi* (a delicate, local white fish) laced with a coconut-infused sauce, kangaroo curry eaten with *chapattis*, or Tasmanian lobster with mango salad are, now, quite the norm, not the exception. If the global palate is going to be a universal one, then Australia is at its very frontier.

1 cup water
1 cup dry white wine
1 bay leaf
2 fresh parsley sprigs
4 peppercorns
1 small brown onion, quartered
1 carrot, peeled and sliced
1 small celery stalk, chopped
¼ tsp salt
court bouillon
500 gm green lobster tails, raw
2 large ripe mangoes,
  peeled and sliced thin

sauce
2 tbsp white wine vinegar
½ cup oil
40 fresh basil leaves
salt and freshly ground pepper
1 clove garlic, finely minced

new zealand

North Island to South Island, New Zealand is renowned for her breathtakingly beautiful and varied scenery. Ideal climate and acres and acres of rich, grazing land have cultivated a burgeoning industry of agriculture, and in particular, cattle and sheep rearing. It is no surprise that farming forms the economic backbone of the country.

The true essence of New Zealand food is steeped in the freshness of its produce and quality of its meats. Lamb and beef specialties like rack of lamb with cranberry and mustard, and roast shoulder of lamb with apricot and thyme stuffing are just two examples of how Kiwis prepare their country's most populous inhabitant. One item that is virtually their national dish is hot beef or lamb pie in flaky pastry, served warm with potato chips, mashed potatoes, peas and gravy. Though historically British in nature, recently New Zealand's cuisine is increasingly inspired by that of Southeast Asia and Europe.

The country is also home to countless streams yielding a wealth of freshwater fish like salmon, rainbow and brown trout and whitebait. New Zealand is also gaining the world's recognition for her white wines, particularly *Chardonnay* and *Sauvignon Blanc*, which are the perfect accompaniment for her seafood.

Dairy products still rank at the top of New Zealand's export list. And this is reflected in the country's affection for desserts. *Pavlova*, is practically recognized as a national dessert. This meringue pastry is filled with the best the country has to offer: whipped cream, strawberries, kiwifruit and passionfruit.

From the alps in the South to the crystal clear lakes in the North, traveling through New Zealand is tantamount to a visit to an unspoiled land. The fresh produce, livestock and rich culinary landscape only make the trip ever more enjoyable.

rosemary and mustard leg of lamb

1 Preheat oven to 200 degrees Celsius. **2** Rub the lamb with olive oil. Combine the mustard, rosemary, salt and pepper, and press onto the surface of the lamb. **3** Put the leg of lamb onto a roasting pan, then into the oven to cook for 25 minutes. **4** Remove from the oven, cover with foil, and allow to rest for at least 10 minutes. **5** Serve with steamed vegetables, potatoes and mint jelly. **6** Serves 6.

1 leg of lamb
1 tbsp olive oil
3 tbsp whole grain mustard
3 tbsp rosemary,
  finely chopped
salt and pepper to taste

africa

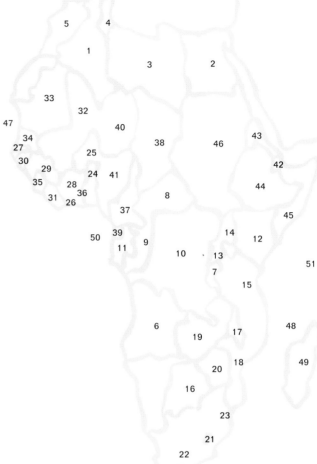

NORTH AFRICA 1 ALGERIA 2 EGYPT

3 LIBYA 4 TUNISIA 5 MOROCCO

CENTRAL AFRICA 6 ANGOLA 7 BURUNDI

8 AFRICAN REPUBLIC 9 CONGO

10 DEMOCRATIC REPUBLIC OF CONGO

11 GABON 12 KENYA 13 RWANDA 14 UGANDA

15 UNITED REPUBLIC OF TANZANIA

SOUTH CENTRAL AFRICA 16 BOTSWANA 17 MALAWI

18 MOZAMBIQUE 19 ZAMBIA 20 ZIMBABWE

SOUTHERN AFRICA 21 LESOTHO

22 SOUTH AFRICA 23 SWAZILAND

WEST AFRICA 24 BENIN 25 BURKINA FASO 26 COTE D'IVOIR

27 GAMBIA 28 GHANA 29 GUINEA 30 GUINEA-BISSAU

31 LIBERIA 32 MALI 33 MAURITANIA 34 SENEGAL

35 SIERRA LEONE 36 TOGO

WEST CENTRAL AFRICA 37 CAMEROON 38 CHAD

39 EQUATORIAL GUINEA 40 NIGER 41 NIGERIA

EAST AFRICA 42 DJIBOUTI 43 ERITREA

44 ETHIOPIA 45 SOMALIA 46 SUDAN

AFRICAN ISLANDS 47 CAPE VERDE

48 COMOROS 49 MADAGASCAR

50 SAO TOME AND PRINCIPE 51 SEYCHELLES

north africa

algeria.egypt.libya.tunisia The food of North African nations share a common heredity dating from their long Islamic history. Once collectively known as the Maghreb, these countries today share similar culinary traditions, albeit with distinctive twists in style and taste preferences.

Tagines (slow-simmered spicy casseroles), *couscous* (steamed semolina grain) and *warka* (a wafer-thin pastry) are distinctive of Algeria, Tunisia and Libya – as is with their North African neighbour, Morocco. Generally, Tunisians prefer their food highly flavoured and spicy. One common element in the food of the three countries is *chermoula*, a distinctive mix of onion, coriander, garlic, chilies and spices used to bring out the character and flavour of many dishes. It is also used as a marinade for grilled, baked or braised fish, poultry, lamb and rabbit. Others include *couscous*; herbs like parsley, coriander and mint; olive oil; spices like cumin, paprika, ginger, cinnamon and cayenne; and *smen*, a preserved clarified butter seasoned with wild herbs, used to add characteristic flavour to *tagines*, *k'dras* and *couscous*.

Beans are as characteristically Egyptian as rice is Asian. A majority of their favourite dishes originate from beans such as *ful medanis* (a brown bean purée made with fava beans), *tameya* (broad bean patties), *ful nabed* (broad bean soup) and *besara* (broad bean purée). *Ful medanis* is served as a *mazza* (appetiser) or as a whole meal with mashed hard-boiled eggs and topped with olive oil, lemon, garlic and flavoured with cumin and parsley. That having been said, Egypt also features many wonderful grilled meat and fish dishes that are taken with rice or *aish*, the ubiquitous Egyptian flat bread.

The cuisine of North Africa is evocative, colourful, sophisticated and rich with the flavours of warm spices. The many similar dishes that transcend geographical boundaries are like related cousins – borne of the same lineage but with distinct personalities of their own.

om ali

250 g *phillo* dough
6 cups fresh milk
½ cup sugar, or according
  to taste
½ cup each of almonds,
  hazelnuts, cashew and raisins
2 tbsp heavy cream or butter

1 Heat oven to about 150 degrees Celsius. Place a sheet of *phillo* dough in it and bake until it turns golden in colour. Take it out, then put another sheet in. Repeat process till all the dough is done. **2** Crush the baked crispy dough in a deep oven-proof bowl. Add the nuts and raisins. **3** Heat the milk separately to just before boiling, and add the sugar. **4** Add half of the milk in the oven-proof bowl, and put it in a 175 degrees Celsius oven for about 15 minutes. **5** Add the rest of the milk, and put the butter or heavy cream on the surface. **6** Put the bowl back in the oven and bake till the top turns golden in colour. Serve warm.

couscous

1 Put meat, two sliced onions, cabbage, half the butter, salt and pepper at the bottom of a *couscous* steamer (*couscousierre*). Pour in the water and bring to boil. **2** Put the upper half of the steamer, containing the *couscous*, over the boiling stock. Allow to cook for half an hour. **3** Once cooked, take the *couscous* off the heat and place in a large deep dish. Press with a ladle to separate the grains. Let the *couscous* air and sprinkle with more water till the grains are swollen. **4** About an hour before serving, put the tomatoes, aubergines, the rest of the onions, carrots, turnip, chilies and coriander in the stock. **5** Cut the pumpkin into quarters and cook separately in a little of the stock. Adjust seasoning to taste. **6** Half an hour before serving put the *couscous* back to steam. **7** When the *couscous* begins to steam, take it off the heat and add the remaining half of the butter. Mix well, and pour on as much of the stock as the couscous can absorb, stirring all the time. **8** Place *couscous* on a large round dish, heaping the grains into a pyramid. **9** Place the meat and vegetables from the stock in a scooped hollow at the top of the *couscous* pyramid. Serve at once. Additional stock may be added if a moister *couscous* is desired.

morocco

Moroccan cuisine hails from refined tradition. A multiple-course authentic Moroccan meal embodies a perfect harmony of colour, flavour and vibrancy, and is truly an experience to savour.

The typical Moroccan dining experience begins with a comfortable setting – usually low round tables on thick-pile carpets and many cushions. The hands (actually the first three fingers and the thumb of the right hand) are often used to eat with in most North African countries and washing them becomes a common precursor to any meal.

Moroccan cuisine is an explosion of tastes, culled from the combination of herbs and spices like ginger, peppers and cumin. *Mezze*, a series of appetisers that come in little plates, are unique to this part of the world and is often the prologue to a feast. *Pastilla*, a pie of *ouarka* pastry similar to *phillo*, layered with almonds and pigeon and topped with cinnamon and sugar, defines what is unique about Moroccan cuisine, a clever mingling of tastes that, more conventionally, seem inappropriate to share the same plate. Similar examples of this interchange of flavours is found in *tajines*, a stew combining meat with vegetables and fruits like prunes, pickled lemons or quince cooked in an earthenware pot over hot coals.

Couscous, of course, is traditionally Moroccan. Steamed semolina accompanied by a light stew of mutton, chicken or vegetables is a staple here, as well as a popular culinary envoy of Moroccan cuisine abroad. Tea spiked with a large sprig of mint is the libation of choice, anytime of day or night.

If a people is judged by the food they eat, then the creativity and imagination of food here speak volumes of the resourcefulness of the Moroccans.

1 kg couscous
1 kg meat, knuckle of veal
    or shoulder of mutton,
    cut into large pieces
1 medium size savoy cabbage, diced
1 kg onions
4 to 5 tomatoes, cut into large pieces
500 g red pumpkin
250 g turnip
250 g aubergine,
    quartered and unpeeled
500 g carrots
2 chilies
1 handful coriander, chopped
300 g butter
1 tbsp pepper
6 litres water
salt to taste

central africa

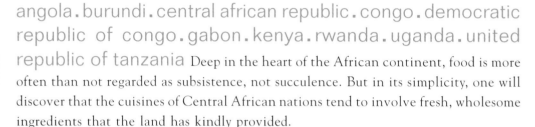
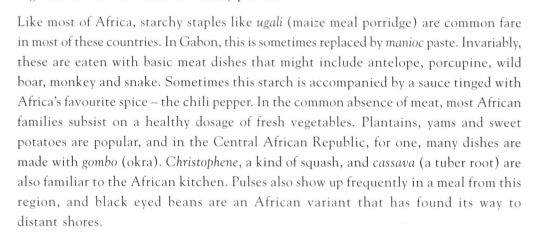
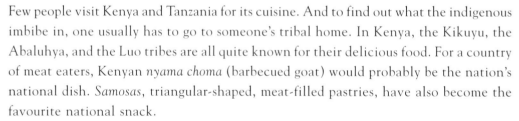

angola.burundi.central african republic.congo.democratic republic of congo.gabon.kenya.rwanda.uganda.united republic of tanzania Deep in the heart of the African continent, food is more often than not regarded as subsistence, not succulence. But in its simplicity, one will discover that the cuisines of Central African nations tend to involve fresh, wholesome ingredients that the land has kindly provided.

Like most of Africa, starchy staples like *ugali* (maize meal porridge) are common fare in most of these countries. In Gabon, this is sometimes replaced by *manioc* paste. Invariably, these are eaten with basic meat dishes that might include antelope, porcupine, wild boar, monkey and snake. Sometimes this starch is accompanied by a sauce tinged with Africa's favourite spice – the chili pepper. In the common absence of meat, most African families subsist on a healthy dosage of fresh vegetables. Plantains, yams and sweet potatoes are popular, and in the Central African Republic, for one, many dishes are made with *gombo* (okra). *Christophene*, a kind of squash, and *cassava* (a tuber root) are also familiar to the African kitchen. Pulses also show up frequently in a meal from this region, and black eyed beans are an African variant that has found its way to distant shores.

Few people visit Kenya and Tanzania for its cuisine. And to find out what the indigenous imbibe in, one usually has to go to someone's tribal home. In Kenya, the Kikuyu, the Abaluhya, and the Luo tribes are all quite known for their delicious food. For a country of meat eaters, Kenyan *nyama choma* (barbecued goat) would probably be the nation's national dish. *Samosas*, triangular-shaped, meat-filled pastries, have also become the favourite national snack.

In Tanzania, the East African influences of coconut-based curries pervade its cuisine. Bananas are freely included in unlikely dishes like meat stews and with fish and poultry. Under the shadow of the towering Kilimanjaro, the romance of Tanzania is epitomized, gastronomically at least, in the Spice Island – Zanzibar. The intoxicating scents of cinnamon and cloves spice the air of this Tanzanian island, and markets are lined with a colourful montage of lemon grass, coconuts, cocoa beans, lichees, and *addoes* (a potato-like vegetable).

samaki wa kusonga
(fish croquettes)

1 Flake the fish coarsely. 2 Add the eggs, salt, saffron, vinegar, red pepper, cumin seed and 4 tbsp of the breadcrumbs. Form into croquettes. 3 Spread the additional cup of breadcrumbs onto a tray and roll the croquettes over it, making sure that the bread-crumbs stick to the surface. Chill in a refrigerator for an hour. 4 Heat the butter in a pan and sauté the croquettes in it till golden brown. 5 Serve with slices of lemon and whole cloves.

500 g cooked fish, halibut,
  flounder, haddock or tuna
  may be used
2 eggs, beaten
1 tsp salt
¼ tsp saffron
1 tbsp vinegar
½ tsp crushed red pepper
¼ tsp of cumin seed
4 tbsp breadcrumbs,
  plus 1 additional cup
2 tbsp butter

garnish
lemon slices and whole cloves

nyama na irio (steak and mashed potatoes)

1½ kg fillet mignon,
  cut into 8 pieces
1 16-oz can of peas
1 16-oz can of kernel corn
4 cups mashed potatoes
3 tbsp butter
1 tsp salt
¼ tsp pepper
oil for frying
6 tbsp flour
2 cups prepared onion soup,
  can be from packet mix
salt and pepper to taste

1 Drain the peas, and put it through a vegetable mill to purée. Save the liquid from the can. 2 Drain the corn, and combine the liquid with that from the peas. 3 Add the butter, salt and pepper to the mashed potatoes and blend well. 4 Blend in the puréed peas until an even green colour is obtained. Fold in the corn and set aside the mixture. 5 Sauté the fillet mignon in a skillet with a little oil until desired doneness. Remove and set aside. 6 Put the flour in the skillet to make a roux with the fat, and then add the onion soup to make a sauce. Add salt and pepper to taste. 7 Return the steak to the sauce and fry briefly to blend. 8 To serve, place the steak onto serving plates and top with sauce. Form a volcano shape with the potato mixture, and pour additional sauce into the hole in the centre. 9 Serves 8.

ugali (cornmeal mush)

This is a staple found throughout the African continent. In Swahili, any thick mush is called ugali. Ugali made from cornmeal is lighter in colour, whereas that made from millet flour tends to be darker. Often, ground peanuts are added to provide flavour.

1 In a large saucepan, bring the water or broth to boil. 2 Add the salt and the cereal. 3 Stir the mixture until it becomes a smooth mush. 4 Before serving, warm in a double boiler to heat.

4 cups water or
  chicken broth
1 tsp salt
1 cup fine white cereal,
  can be farina,
  or cornmeal grits

south central africa

botswana.malawi.mozambique.namibia.zambia.zimbabwe Like many parts of Africa, food in the South Central region of the continent is a result of native evolution and colonial persuasion. From Namibia on the Western coast to Mozambique in the East, the cuisines of these countries share commonalities, albeit tempered and distinguished with characteristic elements.

In the Botswana capital of Gaborone, almost all types of international food may be found. But the true cuisine of this vibrant African nation might be closer found in the heart of the country. Botswana meals are often built around millet and sorghum porridge. In more remote areas, *morama* (a tuber), edible fungus known as *kalahari trufflek*, and the *mopane* worm (that is cooked in hot ash, boiled in salt, or deep-fried) form an interesting round up of bush cuisine. Tribal differences do exist in Botswana gastronomy as well: the Yei of the Okavango like fish; the Herero are partial to dairy; and the Kalanga like their sorghum, millet and maize starches.

Maize meal is also the staple of choice in Malawi, Zimbabwe and Zambia. In Zambia, fish like bream, freshwater salmon and perch are often used in accompanying main dishes. One Malawi variant is *kondowole*, made of cassava flour and slightly rubbery in texture. While in Zimbabwe, meat stews are combined with maize meal porridge to form *sadza ne nyama*. Zimbabwe is also one of the world's largest producers of beef, and fish from Lake Kariba are considered delicacies. True to the British heritage that lines Zimbabwe's history, beer is a favoured drink there and *chibuku* is a local brew that is easily found in local beer halls.

In the same vein, Namibia's colonial past has defined a kindly slant towards many foods and drinks of German origin. Lovers of *boerewors*, (a type of farmers' sausage), cold meats and breads, will not be at a lost in this African nation. For a more colloquial flavour, the desert-inhabiting Nama tribe revere the *nara* melon to the extent that some are convinced man owes his existence to the fruit. Namibia's Ovambo people, on the other hand, are akin to *mielie pap* (maize meal porridge), and *mahango* (millet), eaten with meat and fish dishes.

Like Sao Tome and Principe, Cape Verde, and Angola, the food of Mozambique is steeped in Portuguese traditions. This is evident in a dish called *matata* (clams cooked in port with peanuts and tender greens or fruit). *Frango*, a *calrial* (or curry) is also a national favourite and features chicken rubbed with *piri-piri* (hot peppers) and roasted over charcoals. The influence of India is also obvious in Mozambique cuisine. *Manga achar*, is a kind of mango *chutney* eaten with *calrial*, as are several varieties of *sambals* of Indian origin. The coastal areas in Mozambique are particularly known for shellfish, prawns, fish, and lobster – cooked in a range of ways reflecting the myriad cultures that define this multi-ethnic land.

sadza with beef stew

sadza: **1** Warm the water in a large stew pot and add 2 cups of maize meal. **2** Stir until slightly thickened. **3** Bring to a boil, then add gradually more maize meal and stir until the dough becomes smooth. More water may be added for a smoother, lighter consistency. **beef stew**: **4** Fill a pot with water and bring to a boil. **5** Boil the beef till tender, then remove from the water. **6** In a deep skillet, heat about 3 tbsp of oil. **7** Brown the beef cubes, then add onions and sauté till soft. **8** Add tomatoes and cook for about 3 minutes. **9** Add a cup of water and boil for 5 minutes. If desired, more vegetables (like carrots, turnips, or cauliflower) may be added.

sadza
½ **maize meal**
1 litre water

beef stew
1 kg beef, cut into cubes
4 tomatoes, cut into large pieces
2 onions, cut into large pieces
salt and pepper to taste

chicken yachikasu

2 chickens with skin on, washed, dried and cut into small pieces, and seasoned with salt and pepper
200 ml oil
3 medium tomatoes, chopped
2 medium onions, chopped
4 tbsp curry powder preferably chikasu – a local curry powder
600 ml water

1 Heat oil in a frying pan & stir-fry the chicken pieces till they turn brown. Remove and set aside. **2** In a saucepan, fry the chopped onions till they turn brown; add chopped tomatoes, and cook for 2 – 3 minutes. **3** Add the curry powder or *chikasu* and sauté for 2 – 3 minutes. **4** Add the sautéed chicken and water. Bring to boil, reduce the heat to low and simmer till chicken is cooked, about 10 – 12 minutes. **5** When cooked, transfer to a serving bowl and serve with steamed rice. **6** Serves 4.

matata (clam and peanut stew)

Although the cuisine of Mozambique is greatly influenced by the Portuguese, this typical entrée is one the country can call their own. *Matata* is usually made with pumpkin leaves, but spinach is a good alternative.

1 Sauté the onions with a little olive oil till soft, but not brown. **2** Add the clams, peanuts, tomatoes and season to taste with salt, and black and red pepper. Simmer gently for half an hour. **3** Add the pumpkin leaves or spinach and cook until the leaves are wilted. **4** Serve immediately with white rice. **5** Serves 8.

4 cups clams, chopped
1 cup peanuts, chopped finely
1 cup onions, chopped finely
olive oil for frying
2 tomatoes, chopped
1 kg fresh pumpkin leaves, or spinach, chopped finely
salt, black pepper and crushed red pepper to taste

South Africa is a land of many cultural faces. In and around Cape Town, the large Malay community has carved out an influence now known as Cape Malay. Much of this influence is evident in the food found in South Africa today. For the most part, the origins of *babotie* is that of Cape Malay and has little to do with the food of the indigenous tribes in South Africa. It consists of ground meat (usually mutton or beef), flavoured with curry, apricots, raisins, nuts, and other spices.

babotie

This is a popular dish of Cape Malay origin. It consists of ground meat (usually mutton or beef), flavoured with curry, apricots, raisins, nuts and other spices.

1 Chop the onions and sauté in the oil with curry powder and turmeric. **2** Add the meat and other spices, brown lightly. Transfer to a flat oven-proof dish. **3** Make the custard by beating the eggs, and then adding the milk. Mix in the apricot jam, lemon juice, raisins and apricots. Pour this over the meat and decorate with bay leaves and almonds on top of the mixture. **4** Bake in a medium oven at 180 degrees Celsius for about 45 minutes. **5** Garnish with desiccated coconut, *chutney* and bananas, and serve with rice.

southern africa

Like most of the African continent, maize is a main feature in the diet of the indigenous tribes in southern Africa. Among the South African groups, some interesting dietary departures come to mind. Although something as seemingly bland as *wahobe* (maize cooked with flour and pumpkin) is considered a popular staple, native South Africans are also partial to the likes of *mopale* (worms – dried, then roasted with peanuts and served with a pepper sauce or banana), and roasted locusts.

In Lesotho, *sehewpa* (horse meat) is a popular source of protein. Otherwise, *stiff pap* – roasted cornstarch – is a staple that is also served during festivities and cultural gatherings. Similarly in Swaziland, maize is used to make porridge, sometimes served with a stew.

Immigrant groups like the Portuguese, Greeks and Germans define the food of this country. Around the Cape, the Indian and Dutch have influenced the popularity of well-spiced Indonesian-type dishes. Of these, *bredies* are famous for their fragrant blend of meat, onions, tomatoes, chilies, cabbage and pumpkin. Similarly, in Durban, where a large Indian population resides, hot curries, *beryanis* and *tandoori* meats are the order of the day.

If at all, the Dutch-Afrikaner derived foods distinguish the South African table. These dishes – often featuring fresh game – are hearty and not usually found in restaurants. A typical meal will consist of meat, pumpkin, corn fritters, and mushy vegetables tinged with cinnamon, sage and milk. For more festive occasions, a *braai* features a communal barbecue of well-marinated meats and sausages like *boerewers*, a highly spiced farmer's sausage.

Since the end of apartheid, South African meats, seafood, and fruit have been sought after around the world. Crayfish and abalone harvested from the waters off the Cape are known for their highest quality.

South African wines, though increasing in price, are fast becoming known as the best value for money additions for any cellar around the world. However, if you ask a native, they might be more predisposed towards locally brewed concoctions like *umqombothi* – a beer brewed from maize.

1 kg of ground meat,
  beef or mutton
1 large onion
30 ml oil
15 ml apricot jam
60 ml lemon juice
75 g seedless raisins
10 dried apricots
30 ml curry powder
5 ml turmeric powder
5 ml salt
2 ½ ml black pepper

custard
250 ml milk
2 eggs
15 almonds, sliced
  or crushed
6 bay leaves

garnish
desiccated coconut
chutney
bananas

west africa

benin.burkina faso.cote d'ivoire.gambia.ghana.guinea.
guinea-bissau.liberia.mali.mauritania.senegal.sierra leone.
togo Across the West African stretch of nations, the influences of the French and Islamic cultures are palpable. The food eaten in these countries, similarly, did not escape the throes of colonization or religious evangelism. However, the large number of ethnic groups and tribes that populate this large region has carved out different cuisines that rank as some of the more distinctive in the continent.

Rice, and the starchy African staple of *fou-fou* (made from cassava, manioc, plantains or other root vegetables) are often the foil from which to soak up any West African's favourite sauce. In Burkina Faso, sauce is often the primary attraction that subordinates the common ingredients of rice (as in the dish, sauce with rice or *riz* sauce), vegetables (*riz gras*), fish (*sauce de poisson*), or beef and eggplant (*boeuf sauce aubergine*). Such is also the case in Togo where some of the best West African food is found. Here, the base may be rice, *paté* (made from millet, corn, manioc or yams), *ablo* (made with corn and sugar), or *monple* (made with fermented corn). Togo's coastline gives rise to *lamounou dessi* or *sauce de poisson* (fresh fish sauces), as well as *aglan* (crab). Further inland, *abobo* (snails), *egbo pinon* (smoked goat), and *koklo meme* (grilled chicken with chili sauce) are popular dishes.

Like Togo, a French accent is discernible in the food of Mauritania and Cote D'Ivoire. *Maquis* is typical fare from the Ivory Coast featuring chicken and fish cooked in onions and tomatoes and served with *attieke* (starch made of cassava). On a simpler note, *aloco* is a meal of banana in palm oil, cooked with onions and chili and hawked by street venders. Senegal, despite its strong indigenous culture, has not escaped French influence in its cuisine as well. *Poulet* (grilled chicken), *poisson yassa* (grilled fish), *tieboudienne* (rice with fish and vegetable sauce), and *mafe* (peanut stew) are local dishes whose names evoke a place thousands of miles away. Street hawkers are common in Gambia and offer a wide variety of food that includes *sow* or *kossam* (yogurt) and *latcheri* (ground millet). Otherwise, informal 'chop shops' and roadside shacks called *afra*, generally offer a menu of grilled meats cooked with spices, and rice with a variety of sauces.

nkrumana ntroba froyee
(okra and garden egg stew served with banku)

banku: **1** Put fermented dough in a cooking bowl. Mix with the cassava dough. Add water and stir. **2** Cook over medium heat, stirring constantly. Season with salt to taste. When it thickens, add a little water if a runnier consistency is desired. Set aside. **stew**: **3** Wash beef cubes, trim off any excess fat. Rinse, marinate with a little salt and steam. **4** Clean and wash the dried shrimps thoroughly. Blend onion with ginger and dried shrimps until smooth. **5** Heat oil and fry the onions and shrimp mixture until it is dry, but not burnt. **6** Add chopped tomatoes and continue frying till the mixture is dry. **7** Add chopped beef, fish flakes and ¾ cup stock. Bring to a slow boil. **8** Add the chopped okura and eggplants. Cover and let simmer for about 20 minutes or till vegetables are almost cooked. **9** Season with salt and red chilies and continue simmering until the stew thickens slightly. **10** Serve with *banku*, about 4 portions.

stew
250 g beef, cut into cubes
5 g fresh ginger root
1 large onion,
 cut into large chunks
3 – 4 medium-sized ripe
 tomatoes, skinned and
 chopped fine
100g salted fried codfish
1 cup smoked flaked
 mackerel or tuna
24 fingers of okra, chopped
8 medium-sized
 eggplants, chopped
salt and chopped red chilies
 (optional) to taste
100 g dried shrimps
⅓ cup vegetable oil
¾ cup stock

banku
300 g fermented corn dough
50 g cassava dough
3 cups water

Historical British rule, on the other hand, had a small role to play in Ghanaian cuisine, if anything, to thwart the general sweep of French influence throughout the region's culinary topography. Thick broth-like soups are commonly found, as are peanut stews and *forowe* (fishy tomato stew). *Jollof* rice is an easy one-dish meal while dishes like *gari foto* (egg, onions, dried shrimp and tomatoes) and *kyemgbuma* (crabs with cassava dough, meat and potatoes) are frequent accompaniments to *gari* (a starch made from manioc flour) and the omnipresent African *fou-fou*.

Despite the proliferation of Islam throughout the West African stretch, there is an availability of various types of alcoholic beverages. For the most part, those made from millet and palm are brews of choice among the indigenous. Interestingly, there are many local breweries that make their own beer as well.

okra sauce

1 Cut beef into 2 – 3-cm cubes. **2** Chop okra, eggplants, green peppers and tomatoes into 5-cm cubes. **3** Place beef, mushrooms and onions in a deep casserole. Add the bouillon cubes, then enough water to cover and cook over strong heat until boiling. Reduce heat and continue cooking for 30 minutes. Remove from heat. **4** In another pan, heat the palm oil, add the chopped vegetables and garlic, then fry slowly for 15 minutes. **5** Add the fried vegetables to the beef casserole. Cover and cook for about 15 minutes. **6** Season with salt and pepper. **7** Remove from heat and serve hot with steamed white rice.

100 g beef
5 large mushrooms, sliced
2 onions, sliced
50 g okra
2 eggplants
5 tomatoes, peeled
2 *shishito* (sweet green peppers)
1 garlic clove, chopped finely
2 tbsp palm oil
2 bouillon cubes
salt and black pepper to taste

jollof rice

1 Sauté the meat in about ½ cup of oil till brown. Set aside. **2** In a separate pot, fry the onions, green peppers, ginger in ¼ cup of oil till onions are soft. Add the whole tomatoes and simmer for about 5 minutes. **3** Add the tomato paste, water, salt, black pepper, thyme and red pepper and simmer for another 20 – 25 minutes. **4** In a separate saucepan, cook the rice in the stock. Season to taste. **5** Combine the sauce of the meat with the rice. **6** Put the *jollof rice* in a serving bowl and arrange the meat in the centre. **7** Serves about 8.

Variations of this dish are served throughout West Africa. In Liberia, pig's feet are popularly used, together with salted pork and bacon.

1 kg cooked meat, e.g. chicken,
    shrimp or smoked pork
½ onions, chopped
½ green peppers, chopped
½ tsp ground ginger
1 16-oz can of whole tomatoes
1½ cups tomato paste
8 cups water
1 tbsp salt
½ tsp black pepper
½ tsp thyme
1 tsp crushed red pepper
2 cups white rice, raw
5 cups chicken stock
oil for frying

attieke-fried fish with tomato sauce

1 Mix the *attieke* (casava's *couscous*) with some vegetable oil and salt. Cook in a steamer for 10 minutes. Set aside. **2** Purée the chopped onions, tomatoes, and garlic in a blender. Add chicken bouillon cubes, vegetable oil and the juice from 1 carrot. **3** Put the purée in a pan and cook gently on low heat till all the water from the vegetables is evaporated. Place in a sauceboat. **4** Coat the fish fillets with salt and flour. Deep-fry till golden brown. **5** Serve fried fish fillets with the accompanying tomato sauce and *attieke*.

1 kg sea bream or sea bass, scaled,
    filleted and cut into four pieces
salt, flour and oil for deep frying
attieke (casava's *couscous*)

sauce
4 tomatoes
4 tbsp garlic, chopped
4 tbsp onions, chopped
2 cubes chicken bouillon
4 tbsp vegetable oil
1 carrot, juiced

yassa au poulet de la casamance
(barbecued chicken with lemon and onions over rice)

1 Rub the chicken with the halved lemon, squeezing the juice over it. Marinate with the onions, chopped parsley, black pepper, salt, bay leaves, thyme, crushed red pepper, additional lemon juice and oil, and leave for 30 minutes. **2** Remove the chicken, set the onion marinate aside, and broil till it browns on all sides and is about half cooked. **3** Simmer the onion marinade over heat in a small pot, stirring to prevent it from sticking to the pot. Onions should remain white. Do not cook more than 5 minutes. **4** Bring chicken back to the pan and cover them with the onions. Pour the chicken stock over the chicken and bake in a 180 degrees Celsius oven until the onions turn golden brown. **5** Put chicken pieces onto serving plates and spoon the onion sauce over it. **6** Serve with white rice and garnish with watercress or parsley.

4 1-kg chickens, cut in halves
1 lemon, cut in half
1½ kg white onions, thinly sliced
½ cup parsley, chopped
1 tbsp black pepper
1 tbsp coarse salt
3 bay leaves
1 tsp thyme
1 tsp crushed red pepper
1 cup lemon juice
1 cup oil
1 quart chicken stock

garnish
watercress or parsley

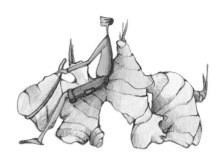

west central africa

cameroon . chad . equatorial guinea . niger . nigeria The West Central region of Africa is a hodgepodge of ethnic diversity tinged with an Anglo-French colonial past. Hundreds of ethnic tribes populate the countries of Equatorial Guinea, Cameroon, Niger, Nigeria and Chad, giving way to a cultural complexity unsurpassed in any other part of the continent. This complexity is compounded by the presence of both Islam and Christianity throughout the region.

Without a doubt, the French probably had a significant influence in the food of Cameroon. Grilled *brochettes* stuffed into *baguettes* with an accompanying salad are often found sold on sidewalks, albeit a little more spiced than one would find in France. Indigenous ingredients are also prepared in a familiarly French style. Manioc leaves, for one, are often used as *feuille* in many dishes. The African mainstay of *couscous*, rice or starch-like carbohydrate, like *pae* or *fufu* (a starchy staple made from rice, corn, manioc, plantains or bananas) doused with sauce is a frequent presence on the Cameroonian table.

In the predominantly Hausa-speaking Niger, regional differences are restricted to yoghurt, mutton and rice in the North, and *couscous* and *ragout* in the South. While in Nigeria, most of what locals like to consume is often found sold at roadside stalls, or *buka*. Likewise, meat such as beef, is found in the North, while well-spiced stews proliferate in the South of the country. Like most of Africa, a meal in Nigeria is built around grain. Notably, *tuwo* is a starch made from maize or millet. *Isi-ewu* (goat head and pepper soup), *egusi* (meat and red pepper stew) and *efo* (a vegetable soup) are main dishes that round out a meal in a country – and region – possessing a cornucopia of cultures and ethnicity.

east africa

Café societies around the world have Ethiopia to thank for their very existence. For it was here that the coffee bean was first discovered and consumed. The Ethiopian word for one of the world's most popular beverages is *buna*, rather unlike any of its international names like coffee, *café*, *kofye*, *kahava*, *kaffa*, etc. However, in the fourteenth century, the drink was taken to Yemen where it acquired the Arabic name, *qahroeh*, possibly a colloquial version of *Kaffa*, the Ethiopian region where the first plants were discovered.

Making coffee in Ethiopia is serious business. The ceremony is a rather formal one where the woman of the household would first make her guests comfortable in her home by burning incense. She would then roast green coffee beans in a pan before pounding them into powder with mortar and pestle. All this is done in front of her visitors. She then infuses the coffee powder into a pot of water before serving.

Ethiopian food is also often eaten in a communal setting. *Injera*, the national pancake-like bread made from *teff* (a local grain), normally forms the centrepiece of a meal. This is eaten with dishes like *wot*, a spicy stew of meat, fish or vegetables prepared with *berbere* (a spicy mélange of red pepper, herbs and spices), or *doro*, a much milder dish of chicken or lamb cooked with onions and green ginger. A dessert of honeycomb and an infusion of *hojja*, a tea made from the dried leaves of the coffee plant, go a long way in tempering the hotness of an Ethiopian meal.

Food in East Africa may be seen as a continuum of the cuisines of the Middle East and the south Mediterranean. Dishes from Djibouti are clear examples of that. Restaurants here serve predominantly French-influenced dishes, while 'street food' is typically North African and is tinged with Arabic flavours. Chicken, fried meats and fish – in particular, Red Sea fish barbecued in a spicy sauce – are common main courses, often served with lentils and flat breads.

1 kg unsalted butter,
  cut into small pieces
1 onion, coarsely chopped
3 tbsp garlic, minced
4 tbsp fresh ginger,
  finely chopped
2 tbsp ground turmeric
¼ tbsp ground cardamom
1 cinnamon stick
  (approximately 3-cm long)
1 whole clove
⅛ tbsp ground nutmeg

niter kebbeh (spiced butter)

1 In a large saucepan, melt butter slowly over medium heat. Bring to a boil without letting it turn brown. **2** Stir in onion, garlic, ginger, turmeric, cardamom, cinnamon, clove and nutmeg. **3** Reduce heat and simmer uncovered and undisturbed for 45 minutes. Milk solids at the bottom should be golden brown and the butter on top should be transparent. **4** Slowly pour the liquid into a bowl, straining through cheesecloth. Be careful not to leave any solids in the *niter kebbeh*. **5** Transfer *niter kebbeh* into a jar, cover tightly and store in the refrigerator.

berbere (spice paste)

1 Toast ginger, cardamom, coriander, fenugreek, nutmeg, cloves, cinnamon and allspice over low heat in a cast-iron skillet. **2** Combine spices, onion, garlic, 1 tablespoon salt and 3 tablespoons water in a blender and blend until smooth. **3** Combine paprika, cayenne pepper, black pepper and remainder of salt in the skillet and toast over low heat for about a minute. **4** Stir in the water, ¼ cup at a time, then stir in blended mixture. **5** Stirring vigorously, cook over lowest possible heat for about 10 – 15 minutes. **6** Transfer *berbere* to a jar, let cool to room temperature before covering with a little oil. **7** Store in refrigerator till ready to use.

1 tsp ground ginger
1 tsp ground cardamom
½ tsp ground coriander
1 tsp ground fenugreek
¼ tsp ground nutmeg
⅛ tsp ground clove
⅛ tsp ground cinnamon
⅛ tsp ground allspice
2 tbsp onion, finely chopped
1 tbsp garlic, minced
2 tbsp salt
2 cups paprika
2 tbsp ground cayenne pepper
½ tsp ground black pepper
1½ cups water
oil

500 g – 1 kg chicken,
   cut into 8 serving pieces
2 tbsp fresh lemon juice
2 tsp salt
2 onions, finely chopped
¼ cups *niter kebbeh*,
   (see accompanying recipe)
3 cloves garlic, minced
1 tsp ginger root, finely chopped
¼ tsp ground fenugreek
¼ tsp ground cardamom
⅛ tsp ground nutmeg
¼ cups *berbere* (see recipe above)
2 tbsp paprika
¼ cup dry red wine
¾ cup water
4 eggs, hard-boiled
black pepper, freshly ground

doro wat (chicken stewed in red pepper paste)

1 Rinse and dry chicken pieces. Rub with lemon juice and salt and let sit at room temperature for 30 minutes. **2** Cook the onions over medium heat for about 5 minutes in a large stewpot. Do not let brown or burn. **3** Stir in the *niter kebbeh*. Add garlic and spices. Stir well. **4** Add the *berbere* and paprika, and sauté for 3 – 4 minutes. **5** Add the wine and water and bring to a boil. Cook briskly, uncovered, for about 5 minutes. **6** Pierce the eggs with a fork, making insertions of about 1cm all over the surface. **7** After the chicken is cooked, add the eggs and turn them gently in the sauce. **8** Cover and cook for an additional 15 minutes. **9** Add pepper to taste.

1 kg chopped beef
8 tomatoes, large and firm
1 cup cooked rice
1 tsp salt
½ tsp pepper
2 cloves garlic, minced
4 tbsp fresh dill, chopped
4 tbsp oil
2 tbsp butter
2 6-oz cans tomato paste
2 cups water
½ tsp salt
1 tsp cinnamon
1 tsp garlic powder

garnish
tomato slices
green olives

maschi (stuffed tomato with chopped beef)

Cucumbers or eggplants may be used instead of tomatoes.

1 Sauté the beef with the minced garlic, salt and pepper with 2 tbsp of oil until the meat browns.
2 Add the cooked rice and blend. **3** Cut a slit in the tomatoes and squeeze the sides to open the slit.
Scoop up the pulp of the tomatoes and stuff with the beef/rice mixture. **4** Heat the butter and 2 tbsp
of oil in a skillet and gently sauté the stuffed tomatoes until they turn dark red in colour. Remove and
place in a saucepan. **5** Combine the tomato paste, water, cinnamon and garlic powder, and season
with salt. **6** Pour over the stuffed tomato and simmer over a gentle heat for 10 – 15 minutes until the
sauce thickens. **7** Remove onto a serving platter and pour the thick sauce over the stuffed tomatoes.
8 Garnish with fresh tomato slices and green olives.

african islands

cape verde.comoros.madagascar.mautitius.sao tome and principe. seychelles A culinary sojourn through the African islands is like travelling through three continents at the same time. European influences pervade by way of the Portuguese in Sao Tome and Principe, to the French of Madagascar, Seychelles and Mauritius. And despite the proximity to the dark continent itself, food here is more swayed by the piquant flavours of India than from its own mainland.

The ethnic hybridity of Comoros typifies this varied culinary scene. Like most of these islands, the population is a rich mix of Africans, Malay-Polynesians (or Malagasy), Arabs and Afro-Eurasians. Food here is a rich palette of Arabic, French, Indian, and of course, African. Seafood is on the main agenda, often spiked with spices like cardamom, coriander, nutmeg, cinnamon and cloves. Those partial to French cuisine should enjoy *langouste a lavanille*, a local delicacy of lobster cooked in vanilla.

Long after the French had left Africa, vestiges of their gastronomic persuasion remained in Madagascar, Mauritius and Seychelles, albeit with local twists. Rice remains the staple of choice in Madagascar and is often the primary constituent in a meal accompanied by small amounts of meat. Other favourites include the Malagasy dishes of *romazaya* (beef and vegetable stew) and *ravitoto* (pork and manioc stew), eaten with a side of *achard* (pickled vegetable curry).

The marriage of many cultures is also seen in the food of the Mauritius. Creole, European, Chinese and Indian tastes collide in an explosion of delicious proportions. Chinese *mine* (pronounced 'min') and fried rice have become common meals. Indian *samosas* and *dhal* (split pea) croquettes are eaten with the French-accented *rougaille* (a tomato filling) to round out an international combo. From the *poisson vindaye* (fish cooked with a mix of mustard, garlic, turmeric and other spices) and *achards legumes* (al dente pickled vegetable) of street vendors, to the restaurant fare of meats and fish cooked as *carri* (curry), *daube* (stewed with vegetables), or *kalya* (cooked with saffron and garlic or ginger), Mauritius cuisine is ever the lively dance to an international beat.

In Seychelles, Creole cuisine is the main deal. Anything that swims may show up on the dining table: shark, barracuda, kingfish, squid and parrot fish are all free game, cooked Creole style in a mélange of spices and herbs. Octopus is a real treat and may be served cold in a cocktail or hot in a creamy coconut curry. Shellfish are not safe from the Seychellois palate, and *tec-tec* (tiny white shells) are scrounged up and made into a favourite soup. As with the rest of the countries, fresh fruits are one of the main features among the isles. In the Seychelles, however, breadfruit stars in a legend whereby anyone eating it is destined to return to this island paradise. As much as the French had their say in what African islanders eat, the Portuguese also had their influence, but more specifically in Cape Verde and Sao Tome and Principe. Dishes like *pastel com diablo dentro* (pastry filled with tuna), *bananas enroladas* (deep-fried banana in pastry) and *coldo de peixe* (fish stew) reek of flavours usually associated with a country several thousand kilometers north.

Despite some Islamic affinity among the islands, local alcoholic drinks are present and offer a colourful display of creativity. *Toaka grasy* (from rice and sugar cane), *litchel* (from lychees) and *trembo* (coconut toddy) are commonly found in Madagascar, which also produces several excellent wines from Ambalayao and Fianarantsoa. Less potent libations are found vis-à-vis the *lassi* (yoghurt drink) and *alouda* (*agar* milk drink) of Mauritius. Unavoidably, any selection of food or drink throughout these islands will unveil a multi-ethnic blend touched upon by history and imagination.

varenga (roast shredded beef)

1 In a large pot, put in the beef, water, garlic, onion and salt. Bring to a boil and then lower the heat. Simmer for about 2 hours or until the beef is fork tender. **2** Remove the meat and shred. Transfer shredded beef onto a baking pan and roast for 30 minutes in an oven heated to about 185 degrees Celsius. Beef should be lightly browned at the top. **3** Garnish with parsley and serve with white rice. **4** Makes about 6 – 8 servings.

2 kg beef, cut into strips
4 cups water
1 cup onion, sliced
2 tbsp salt
3 cloves garlic, chopped finely

garnish
parsley

shark chutney

1 Finely mash the cooked shark and drain. Squeeze *bilimbi* juice and add to the shark. 2 Mix onion, pepper, salt and turmeric. Heat the oil and fry the onion mixture for 3 minutes. 3 Add the shark and fry for another 5 minutes. 4 Mix in the juice of the lime before serving with boiled cassavas.

1 kg shark, boiled
  with skin removed
2 *bilimbi* (an indigenous
  tropical fruit), sliced
1 lime, halved
2 tsp vegetable oil
1 tsp turmeric
onion
pepper
salt

ladob

2 green *St. Jacques* bananas
2 medium-sized sweet
  potatoes
3 coconuts, grated, soaked
  in 3 cups of warm water
250 g sugar
pinch of grated nutmeg
1 vanilla pod, finely chopped

1 Peel and slice the bananas and the sweet potatoes. Place in a large, heavy-bottomed saucepan. Sprinkle on the sugar, nutmeg and the vanilla pod. 2 Squeeze the grated coconut by hand to extract enough milk to cover the fruit. Bring to a boil slowly, stirring constantly, and then simmer till the fruit is soft and the sauce is creamy. 3 Serve hot or cold as a dessert.

1½ kg beef bones
8 cups water
1 small turnip, cut into
  medium-sized pieces
3 carrots, cut into pieces
8 scallions, cut into pieces
1 cup string beans
1 cup tomatoes, quartered
salt and black pepper to taste

lasopy (vegetable soup)

1 Bring water to a boil, put in a little salt and then add the beef bones. 2 Put in the vegetables and a little black pepper to taste. Simmer for about an hour or till the vegetables are tender. 3 Remove the beef bones and process the vegetables and soup till it forms a thick puree. 4 Reheat the thick soup before serving. 5 Makes about 6 – 8 servings.

middleeast

1 IRAN 2 IRAQ 3 ISREAL

ARABIA 4 BAHRAIN

5 KUWAIT 6 OMAN

7 QATAR 8 SAUDI ARABIA

9 UNITED ARAB EMIRATES

MID-EAST 10 JORDON

11 LEBANON

12 SYRIAN ARAB REPUBLIC

13 YEMEN

iran & iraq

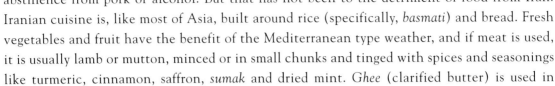

Islamic predominance in this part of the world has meant strict abstinence from pork or alcohol. But that has not been to the detriment of food from Iran. Iranian cuisine is, like most of Asia, built around rice (specifically, *basmati*) and bread. Fresh vegetables and fruit have the benefit of the Mediterranean type weather, and if meat is used, it is usually lamb or mutton, minced or in small chunks and tinged with spices and seasonings like turmeric, cinnamon, saffron, *sumak* and dried mint. *Ghee* (clarified butter) is used in place of cooking oil and *limu omani* (dried lime) is often used whole in many dishes.

An Iranian favourite is *chelou kebab*, a simple dish comprising rice and lean lamb, thinly sliced and marinated in lemon and onion juice, and then charcoal-grilled. The rice is served with butter, *sumak* and raw egg yolk. Other common dishes include *khoresh*, a combination of meat or poultry with vegetables, a sauce of fruit and spices, served with rice dishes, *abgusht* (a meat stew) and *mast va khiar* (yoghurt and cucumber salad). A variety of breads like *nane lavash*, *taftoon*, *sangkyak* and *barbari* form part of every meal. And the usual accompanying refreshment is *chay* (tea), served scalding hot, black and strong, and drunk with a lump of sugar held between the teeth.

As in Iran, lamb, beef and chicken are key ingredients of Iraqi cuisine. Similarly, *basmati* rice is a common staple. As much as the cuisines of both nations resemble each other, distinctions prevail with regards to preparation concept and presentation. *Baharat* (a spice mix found only in the Gulf States), all spice, pepper and *paprika* form the usual suspects in food flavourings. And it is not uncommon to find *rashad* and *barbeen* (cress-like herbs), dried dates, rose water, orange flower water, saffron, walnuts, almonds and *noomi* (dried lime) giving a dish a particular personality.

One would hardly come away from an Iraqi festive meal hungry. The characteristic abundance of varied dishes often run the gamut of the country's favourites: *murag* (a meat stew with okra, eggplant, green peas or beans), roast chicken served with *batata charp* (meat stuffed potato cakes), or salad made with *cos* (romaine) lettuce dressed with date vinegar are popularly served with an accompaniment of *khoubiz* (Iraqi flat bread). Typical of this region in the world, a meal is never complete without strong coffee and sweet pastries.

khobzi (middle eastern flatbread)

Khobzi is a great favourite in the Middle East and accompanies most meals. It is delicious with *hummus* or eggplant seasoned with sesame puree.

1 Dissolve yeast in ¼ cup of the water and sugar, stir and set aside till froth forms, about 10 minutes. **2** Sift the flour and salt into a large bowl. Make a well in the centre of the flour and pour in the yeast mixture. Mix well, adding the remaining water gradually. Knead into a soft dough. **3** Add the oil to the dough and roll into a large ball. Leave dough in the bowl, covered with cloth in a warm draft-free place till it doubles in size, about 2 hours. **4** Pre-heat oven to 230 degrees Celsius. **5** Punch dough down in the centre and roll it out on a floured pastry board. Divide into 8 portions, and roll each portion to a round shape about 6 mm in thickness. Place dough rounds on a lightly floured cloth and allow to rise for another 25 minutes. **6** Place dough rounds on a baking tray and bake in the oven for 4 – 5 minutes, or until golden brown. **7** Remove and wrap in cloth to keep soft till ready to use.

3 cups flour
½ tbsp dry yeast
1 cup lukewarm water
¾ tsp salt
½ tsp sugar
1 tbsp oil

chicken braised in cider

1 Divide sage leaves into equal portions and put into the cavity of the birds. **2** In a large flameproof casserole, melt the fat over a high flame. Brown the birds well in the fat, then remove them and reduce the flame. **3** Add the onion, carrot and turnip, cover and cook for 5 minutes. **4** Place the birds on the vegetables, and then pour in the cider. Bring to a boil, add the bouquet *garni*, cover and transfer to an oven heated to about 150 degrees Celsius. Bake for 2 hours. **5** Remove the birds from the casserole and set aside, keeping them warm. Strain the liquids in the casserole, pressing down on the vegetables to squeeze out all the moisture. **6** Place the birds on a serving platter, pour some of the juices over them and sprinkle with parsley. **7** Serve the remaining juices separately.

israel
Israel's colourful past, and multi-cultural present, has had tremendous influence on the country's cuisine. In this religious centre of three of the world's main religions – Judaism, Christianity and Islam – is seen a convergence of culinary plurality.

The diet of the Jews is dictated, to some extent, by their religious laws. Strict Jewish tradition demands that food is *kosher*, that is, abiding by a rigorous set of rules that regulate how food should be prepared or eaten. Jewish dishes like *gefilte fish* (dumplings made with whitefish), *schnitzel* (veal, turkey or chicken steaks with a crust of *matza* meal – a kind of unleavened flatbread), and *kneidels* (*matza* meal dumplings in chicken soup) are cooked by methods and in utensils that conform to Judaic traditions.

Lunch is often the main meal of the day. But for a quick meal on the run, food from cheap street vendors is quite the norm. In these instances, *falafel* (spiced chickpea fritters) accompanied by *tchina* (chili sauce), and *burekas* (cheese and potato stuffed puff pastry triangles) are ubiquitous items around the country. Arabic and Turkish culinary traditions are also well represented in Israel. *Mezze* (appetisers), *hummus* (spiced chickpea paste), *shawarma* (slices of marinated lamb or chicken cooked in a vertical pit like a *doner kebab*), and *shashlik* (meat *kebabs*) are examples of how Arabic and Turkish food traditions have come to earn an Israeli identity. The wine scene is relatively new in Israel, but the *Golan Cabernet Blanc*, a refreshing white wine that looks rosé, just might be a gem in the making.

The political turmoil in this beautiful, historic country has done little to alter the country's food map. In fact, the racial balance that exists has contributed in a major way to the diverse make-up of Israel's national cuisine.

8 small sage leaves
2 small chickens
(or substitute for 4
pigeons or game hens)
2 tbsp chicken fat
1 medium onion,
chopped coarsely
1 carrot, chopped coarsely
1 small turnip,
chopped coarsely
2 cups apple cider or
apple juice
1 bouquet *garni* of 3 sprigs
parsley, 2 sprigs thyme and
½ bay leaf tied together
¼ cup parsley, chopped

WHAT IS KOSHER?

The word *kosher* is Hebrew for what is 'permitted or allowed', as it relates to consumables. But where did it all began and why? Well, the beginnings of *kosher* laws have their origins in biblical history. They were expounded by Jewish Rabbinic legislation through which the *rabbis* (religious Jewish leaders) interpreted these regulations and applied them to secular life. These laws are found in the *Shulchan Aruch* (Code of Jewish Law) and are discussed in detail in ancient, as well as contemporary writings of the *rabbis*.

That having said, it does little to help the layman determine what is *kosher* or not. Here is a brief primer on the do's and don'ts of *kosher* food.

* Only mammals who chew their curd and are cloven hoofed may be eaten.
* Fish eaten must have fins and scales, and cannot be eaten with meat.
* No shellfish is allowed.
* Only a trained, and certified by rabbinic authorities, butcher is qualified to slaughter animals.
* No blood from any animal may be consumed.
* Meat and milk cannot be eaten together.
* Bread may not be baked with dairy ingredients.

Please note that this is by no means an exhaustive list. Strict kosher laws are extensive and often require rabbinic authority to determine conformity.

maj bus (meat rice)

1 Clean the rice and submerge in water for 30 minutes. **2** Fry the garlic and onions till a little brown. Put in the remaining spices and continue to fry. **3** Add a little water and put the meat in with the spice mixture. Stir until fragrant. **4** Add the water and boil for 30 minutes. Add the bouillon cube, stirring till it is dissolved. Drain the rice and put it in with the meat mixture. **5** Simmer until the rice is fully cooked.

1 kg *basmati* rice
½ kg mutton or chicken, cut into
  small pieces
½ litre water
1 onion, chopped
2 cloves garlic, chopped
1 bouillon cube
1 tbsp *garam marsala* powder
1 tbsp ground coriander
1 tbsp ground dried lemon (black)
1 tsp cinnamon
salt and pepper to taste

najdi meat kabsah

1 Wash the meat well. Heat butter in a saucepan, fry the onions, spices, meat and mix well until the liquid is absorbed. **2** Add the tomatoes, tomato puree. Add the hot water, leave till meat is cooked, then add salt. **3** Wash the rice and pour over the meat. Stir and leave on slow heat till cooked. **4** For the vegetable mixture: Fry onions in the oil till it turns golden brown. Add the spices, stir, then add the tomatoes, tomato puree and broth cube. Cook slowly till all the liquid is absorbed. **5** To serve, place the rice in a serving dish and put onion mixture and meat on top. **6** Garnish with fresh tomatoes, eggs and parsley.

arabia

Mere words can hardly do justice to the famed tradition for hospitality and the impressive cuisine in the Gulf States. Arabic food is often associated only with the boiled meat and spiced rice diet of their nomadic Bedouin people, but this is an overly simplistic view.

The Arab world, stretching from the Levant areas of Lebanon, Syria, Jordan and Palestine to the Gulf States of Saudi Arabia, Oman, Qatar and the United Arab Emirates, has greatly benefited from the spice trade routes established between the East and West. A taste of any of its countless and colourful aromatic rice dishes, enlivened with an assortment of spices, is enough to conjure an image of a bygone trading show voyaging the ancient spice routes.

Since ancient times, skewers of meat paste (*kabab mashwi*) or cubes of tender lamb, served with a salad, have been favorites all over Arabia. But on festive occasions such as weddings, the locals serve up *khouzi*, a whole marinated lamb stuffed with a whole chicken and spiced rice. The khouzi is prepared and roasted until it is so tender that the meat simply falls off the bone. It is served with great pomp and ceremony – with the stuffing spread out on a platter and the lamb resting regally on top.

Bread (*khoubz*) can be found at any Arabian table, from great feasts to the most humble of meals. *Pitta* bread (*khoubz Arabi*) is very popular as is the paper-thin *shraak* used in layering and wrapping foods. Onions, herbs and spices turn the bread into delicious morsels in their own right. Rather than be encumbered with forks and knives, many eat using the fingers of the right hand and use chunks of khoubz as utensils to elegantly collect the food before sliding it into the mouth.

After dinner, mouthfuls of traditional coffee laced with cardamom are served in cups without handles. Served without sugar, it is poured from a silver or brass pot and your cup will be refilled until you make the proper gesture that you have had enough – hold the cup out and cover it with your hand. Remember – it is good etiquette to repay the famous hospitality by having at least three cups. Prepare to follow this with tea *ad infinitum*, deep into the Arabian nights.

2 lamb shoulders,
   cut into 2 pieces
5 cups rice
4 onions, minced
4 tomatoes, coarsely chopped
1 tbsp tomato puree
1 tsp ground spices
   (mixture of black pepper,
   cumin and cardamom)
½ tsp ground spices
   (canella, dried lemon and clove)
¾ cup butter
1½ tbsp salt, or to taste
13 cups hot water

vegetable mixture
5 onions, minced
2 tomatoes, coarsely chopped
½ tbsp tomato puree
½ tsp ground spices
   (black pepper, cumin, canella,
   dried lemon, saffron and
   safflower)
½ cup oil
1 broth cube

garnish
fresh tomatoes, sliced
hard-boiled eggs, sliced
parsley

mid-east

For thousands of years, Syria, Lebanon and Jordan played a significant role as the trading link between and the East and West and, thus, created a melting pot of cultures. As such, their cuisine is the result of a wide variety of foods and diverse nature of people from cities to the deserts.

Generally, Middle Eastern food is sophisticated and elaborate, and is deemed as one of the finest cuisines in the world. Key ingredients found in their food include grain, cheese, yoghurt, *tahini* (a paste made from toasted sesame seeds), fresh and dried fruit, and vegetables. As these are Muslim nations, lamb and chicken are preferred meats, and pork is never used. Game birds such as larks, partridge and pheasant pose a unique alternative. Spices like parsley, mint, cinnamon and allspice are often blended and used in many dishes.

Mezze (appetisers) form an important part of their dining experience. It is not uncommon to find more than ten appetisers at the start of a meal, including *fatayer, sfiha* and *lahm bi'Ajeen* (flat or shaped lamb pies and rolls, and spinach pies, served with the ubiquitous yoghurt or lemon wedges), *labneh makbus* (yoghurt cheese balls), *tabouleh* (salad), *falafel* (dried bean croquettes), and fried or baked *kibbi* balls. All *mezze* are served with *khoubiz*, the Arabic flat bread.

In Jordan, one must try *mansaf* (lamb seasoned with aromatic herbs, sometimes lightly spiced, cooked in yoghurt and served with rice) and baby lamb stuffed with rice, chopped onions, nuts and raisins. Specialties in Lebanon include *kibbeh* (a well-seasoned mixture of finely minced lamb, *bulgur* and chopped onion), either in the form of *kibbeh rass* (balls) or *kibbeh bilsaniyeh* (a pie). If one were to try chicken, the perennial favourites would be *d'jej mohammar ma batatah* (chicken braised with potatoes) and *farrooj meshwi* (grilled chicken). Larks or sparrows are cleaned and grilled over an open fire like *kebabs* or fried and seasoned with lemon juice. Other game consumed includes partridge, pheasant and wild quail accompanied by *toom* (a dip made with garlic, lemon juice and olive oil). *Al-mukhallat* (pickles) are an essential part of the Lebanese life, and they are usually served with olives, bread and fresh salad ingredients. The pickles comprise eggplant, cucumber, chilli peppers and turnip soaked in a solution of salt, sugar, vinegar and water. The Middle Eastern rarely finish their meals with a dessert, but usually have fresh fruit with coffee.

People of Yemen are said to have the distinction of liking spicy foods. This is evident in *shalta*, a fiery stew of lamb or chicken with lentils and spices served over rice. *Zhug* is a popular relish of chilies and pepper flavoured with spices and is used as a bread dip. Breads and cereals are the staples of Yemen. *Malvj* (barley bread) and *bint-al-sahn* (yeast bread fashioned into thin leaves) are two varieties commonly found. Little food is wasted from the Yemeni table. Leftovers are often thrown together to make *hilbeh*, a *fenugreek*-flavoured mixture of rice, vegetables and meat best scooped up with fresh *malvj* bread. Though areas like Moccha are famous for coffee, Yemenis often grind coffee husks and make a drink called *qishr* with ground ginger.

kibbi samak (fish kibbe)

1 Remove skin and any bones from fish. **2** Place fish, onion and *burghul* in a food processor. Add coriander, lemon rind, salt and pepper. While mixing, add the crushed ice cubes gradually so that mixture binds. **3** Place chopped onions and other filling ingredients in the bottom of a round baking dish and microwave at HIGH for 4 – 5 minutes. **4** Allow to cool for a few minutes, then spread the fish mixture evenly on top of the filling. Microwave HIGH for 6 – 8 minutes. Do not overcook. **5** Cut the *kibbe* with a thin pointed knife into eight equal triangles. **6** Running the knife down the middle, cut to the bottom of the baking dish. Then cut each triangle into diamond shapes. Run the knife all around the tray to release the edges. Make a well with a finger in the centre of the dish and sprinkle oil over the surface. Garnish with parsley and lemon slices. **7** Serves 6 – 8.

JORDANIAN TRADITION IN A CUP

Starbucks step aside. Coffee is serious business in Jordan, among the Bedouins at least. For these nomadic inhabitants of the desert, coffee is symbolic to say the least – it signifies hospitality, and at times, even hostility.

For the people of the Badia – the large semi-arid land mass that makes up 80% of Jordan – offering a cup of coffee is synonymous with saying 'hello', or in this case, 'Salaam alaykum; Ahlan wa sahlan'. Communal consumption is considered a symbol of unity, trust and harmony. Naturally, turning down this welcome brew is a customary no-no.

Even the making of the drink is an elaborate affair. Top quality beans are roasted over fire via a long-handled metal spoon called a *mihmas*. It is then cooled in a wooden scoop called a *mibradi*, and pounded with a *mihbash*, a sort of mortar and pestle. The *mihbash* beats out a call to everyone to descend upon the visitor in greeting. The pounded coffee is then boiled in a *dallah* (pot) over charcoal. Cardamom is added before serving to the visitor.

Coffee is almost always served from a brass pot with a curved spout, and poured from the left hand of the server. Had enough? No need to say a word. Just hold your empty cup out with your right hand and wiggle it from side to side.

Usually, the host provides up to three toasts. *Finjan al dayf* ('the guest cup') is the first to welcome the visitor and to establish trust. *Finjan al sayf* ('the sword cup') is the second to symbolise the resolution of any conflicting affairs. Finally, the third one is *'finjan al kayf'* ('the pleasure cup'), solely for the enjoyment of the drink.

As much as coffee is a symbol of harmony, it can also be turned into a knife of dissent. Anybody cheesed off with another only need to spill a cup in front of the other to kick off a ruckus. Often these disagreements need to be settled by sheikhs experienced in tribal customary laws. Worth a thought the next time you order a double-decaf non-fat mocha with whipped cream.

kibbe
250 g white fish fillets
1½ cups fine *burghul*,
   rinsed and squeezed dry
1 onion
1¼ tsp salt
¼ tsp white pepper
¼ cup fresh coriander, chopped
1 tsp lemon rind
4 ice cubes, crushed

filling
2 tbsp vegetable or olive oil
1 small onion, chopped coarsely
¼ tsp salt
a pinch of white pepper
a pinch of turmeric

finish
2 tbsp vegetable or olive oil

garnish
2 – 3 sprigs of parsley
4 – 5 slices of lemon

eastern
europe

EASTERN EUROPE 1 BULGARIA

2 CZECH REPUBLIC 3 ROMANIA

4 SLOVAKIA 5 HUNGARY 6 POLAND

BALTIC STATES 7 BELARUS 8 ESTONIA

9 LATVIA 10 LITHUANIA 11 MOLDOVA

12 RUSSIAN FEDERATION 13 UKRAINE

BALKANS 14 ALBANIA

15 BOSNIA-HERCEGOVINA

16 CROATIA 17 MACEDONIA

18 SLOVENIA 19 YUGOSLAVIA

SOUTH EASTERN EUROPE

20 ARMENIA 21 AZERBAIJAN

22 GEORGIA 23 TURKEY

eastern europe

bulgaria.czech republic.romania.slovakia Eastern European cuisines are influenced greatly by the proximity of neighbouring countries; their varied, often rugged landscape; and a plurality of religious affinities. In particular, moving from the Czech Republic in the heart of the Eastern bloc, through Romania and into Bulgaria, we can easily see the shifts in dietary preference from a European base to one that is tinged with flavours from the East.

After its amicable split with Slovakia, the Czech Republic is slowly coming into its own. Prague, its capital, is earning a reputation not so much for its beauty, but its growing cosmopolitan disposition. Franz Kafka's hometown is quickly seeing a proliferation of restaurants introducing global cuisine to what was a city behind the iron curtain. Typically, however, Czech food is far from the international fare found in the capital city. Dumplings and potato derivatives are a favourite and meat is featured frequently at meals, often dressed heavily with thick, rich sauces. Czech cuisine is accented with German, Hungarian and Polish influences. As such, vegetables are usually well cooked and *sauerkraut* is a usual accompaniment. *Knedlo-zelo-vepro* (dumplings, *sauerkraut* and roast pork) commonly represents itself as a standard, quick meal. Caraway seed, bacon and a zealous salt spoon are often the characteristics of most dishes in the Czech Republic and Slovakia, and potatoes, cabbage, legumes and milk are frequent ingredients used. Regionally speaking, *sauerkraut*, tripe and dense pea soups are popular in the west of Slovakia, while central Slovaks prefer *demikat* (sheep-cheese soup). Other Slovak dishes include *bryndzove halusky* (potato dumplings with sheep's cheese sauce and bacon fat), *vyprazany syr* (fried cheese served with french fries and tartar sauce), *vyprazane reze* (breaded *schnitzel*) and *gulas* (*goulash*) served with *knedliky* (steamed bread).

As Eastern Europe's largest country, the varied geography of Romania influences greatly the food it produces. The hills and plateaus making up a third of the country are populated by orchards and vineyards; and in the fertile plains, cereals, vegetables and herbs find an agreeable abode. Still, Romanian food is known for its consistency more than anything else. Grilled pork, chicken, tripe soup and potatoes are common fare. *Ciorba* (a soup) and *mamagliga* (cornmeal mush that is boiled, baked or fried) often creep into one's daily meal. Perhaps one characteristic of Romanian cuisine is the inclination for sweets. *Placinta* (turnovers), *clarite* (crepes) and *saraille* (almond cake soaked in syrup) offer a highlight to a meal's end. Romanian wines are increasingly known for their value. Alternatively, *tuica* (plum brandy) and *palinca* are liqueurs taken at the beginning of a meal to the cheer of "Noroc!"

Bulgarian meals are similar in a sense that meat and potatoes are a main feature, accompanied by a crisp salad to provide a refreshing refrain. Here, *banitsi* (cheese pastries) is an example of how a food does not have to be complicated to be delicious. It is often eaten with *boza*, a millet drink. For a stronger kick, Bulgarians are partial to either *rakia* or *mastika*, two potent alcoholic libations. From the great Danube, across the Balkan mountain range, to the Aegean and Black Sea coastlines, Bulgaria sits where Europe ends and Asia begins. And her food, more likely than not, reflects this unique disposition.

peceny kapr s kyselou omackou
(carp with sour cream sauce)

1 Grease a shallow dish with butter. Season the carp inside and out with salt and pepper. 2 Place bay leaves on butter, then lay it over the carp. 3 Cover with sour cream and lemon juice. 4 Bake in a 175 degrees Celsius oven, basting frequently, for 40 minutes or till nicely browned. 5 Serve with noodles or potatoes. 6 Serves 4.

¼ cup butter
2 bay leaves
⅓ cup sour cream
1 lemon, juiced
1 carp, about
   1½ – 2 kg, cleaned
salt and pepper

potato noodles with poppy seeds

2 kg potatoes
30 g salt
2 eggs, beaten
250 g semolina flour
500 g corn flour
300 g poppy seeds
300 g powdered sugar
300 g butter

Most families often serve noodles with poppy seeds at the eve of Christmas. The seeds are symbolic of wealth, hence the saying, 'to have such a lot of money as poppy seeds'.

1 Boil potatoes in their jackets, peel them and let them cool. 2 Mash the potatoes thoroughly, add salt, sieved semolina flour, eggs and corn flour (leaving about 50 g to powder the dough). Mix well until you get dough soft enough to roll. 3 Make thick rolls with the dough and cut them to finger size. Using your palm, roll these finger-sized thick rolls into thinner, longer noodles. 4 Cook noodles in slightly salted water. Stir the noodles after putting them in the water so they do not stick to the bottom. 5 When the noodles are cooked, about 10 – 15 minutes, drain them and sprinkle poppy seeds. 6 Serve with powdered sugar and melted butter. 7 Serves 10.

houskove knedliky (bun dumplings)

1 Cut buns, horns or white bread into small croutons. If fresh bread is used, toast it first. 2 Mix *farina* or flour with water, milk, eggs and salt. Keep adding *farina* until dough is smooth and bubbles form, and making sure that it doesn't stick to the bowl. 3 Mix in croutons. 4 Divide into 4 elongated portions. Let sit for about 30 minutes. 5 Place into salted boiling water and cook for about 25 minutes. 6 Remove, drain and cut into smaller sized dumplings with string.

500 g *farina* or flour
2 cups lukewarm water
1 cup milk
2 – 3 eggs
1 tbsp salt
5 large buns, horns or
   white bread

The Russian Federation is the biggest part of former Russia, later the USSR, which also included Ukraine, Belarus, Moldova, and the Baltic Republics of Estonia, Latvia and Lithuania.

In the Russian Federation itself, meat is not consumed in up to 200 fasting days a year. This practice says something about the food in this region. Fish and mushroom are the obvious alternatives, and sturgeons from the Great Volga River are world-famous. Signature dishes of Russia include *blini* (with smoked fish and caviar), *kulebiaka* (layers of sturgeon or salmon, rice, eggs, mushrooms, chicken and game), *pirog* (a large pie filled with meat, cabbage or wild mushrooms) and *pozharsky* (chicken cutlets).

Supplying a large part of Europe's grains has earned Ukraine the title, 'breadbasket of the USSR'. Ukrainian food is honest, hearty and possessing of a home-style quality. The familiar *borshch* (a one-dish soup of red beet and pork or ham, served with sour cream) is arguably a national dish. Other dishes of Ukrainian distinction include *vareniki* (dumplings filled with cottage cheese, *sauerkraut*, chopped liver, sautéed mushrooms, potatoes or fresh sour cherries) and *bigos* (a savoury stew of *sauerkraut* and sausage or pork). Healthy cooking is not high on the Ukrainian's priority list judging from the popularity of *salo* (pig fat) and the plentiful consumption of alcohol, most common of which is *vodka* made from wheat, rye or potatoes.

The Belarussians love their mushrooms, and popular dishes include *hrybi v smetane* (mushrooms with sour cream) and *kotleta po-krestiansky* (pork cutlet with mushroom sauce), downed with *kvas* (a flavoured drink made of malt flour, sugar, mint and fruit). The Moldavians, on the other hand, are fans of *tochitura Moldoveneasca* (pan-fried pork in a spicy pepper sauce topped with a fried egg), dumplings in mushroom sauce and Jewish stews.

Scandinavian influence has lent the Estonian diet its simplicity and an affinity to fish, dairy products and grains. *Kalapirukat* (a closed pie made of rye flour and containing bacon fat, pork and pickled smelts) can be considered a national dish here. Latvians and Lithuanians enjoy stuffed dishes like *varetinai* (potato filled dumplings) and *ristinai* (stuffed beef or pork rolls), *cepelinai* (zeppelin-shaped parcel of potato dough with cheese, meat or mushrooms in the middle). A popular meal of sausages accompanied by *stakliskes* (a honey liqueur) and beer is seldom turned down.

Wars and political reshufflings over the last few centuries have propagated numerous changes in the Russian political landscape. One thing that has remained the same is the rich history of cuisines defining the different cultures of the Russian people.

½ cup lukewarm
     water (40 – 110°C)
3 tsp active dry yeast
2½ – 3 cups
     all-purpose flour
2 cups lukewarm milk
3 eggs, yolks and
     whites separated
½ tsp salt
1 tsp sugar
1 cup butter, melted
     and cooled
3 tbsp cream

blini

The distinctive flavour in *blini* comes from the use of yeast batter. Preparation for this dish should begin about two hours before serving. Once the batter is complete, the *blini* must be cooked and served at once.

1 Pour the lukewarm water into a bowl. Sprinkle the yeast over it, then stir to dissolve completely. Set in a warm, draft-free place for five minutes. **2** Put the flour in a large mixing bowl, make a well in the centre and pour in the yeast mixture and 1 cup of the lukewarm milk. **3** Slowly stir the flour into the liquid ingredients with a wooden spoon, then beat until the mixture is smooth. Cover the bowl with a towel and set it aside in the warm draft-free place for 1 hour. **4** Stir the batter and beat in the remaining cup of lukewarm milk, 3 egg yolks, salt, sugar, 3 tbsp of the melted butter and 3 tbsp of cream. Cover with a towel and let the batter rest in a warm place for another 1 hour. **5** Beat the egg whites until stiff peaks are formed. Fold the whites gently but thoroughly into the batter, cover and let rest in a warm place for 30 minutes. **6** Heat a 30-cm heavy-based pan, with a pastry brush, lightly coat the bottom of it with melted butter. Set the pan over high heat until a drop of water flicked across its surface evaporates instantly. **7** Pour in 4 tbsp of the batter, spread to cover the bottom of the pan. Cook until browned underneath, turn, brown the other side. **8** Repeat with the remaining butter and batter. **9** Before serving, brush the tops of the *blini* lightly with butter. Serve the *blini* hot, accompanied by a bowl of sour cream, caviar or smoked fish. Traditionally, *blini* are spread with butter, then topped with caviar and rolled up. **10** Makes about 1 dozen 30-cm *blini*.

500 g veal meat with bones
500 g red beet root,
   finely chopped
4 tomatoes
400 g cabbage,
   cut into small pieces
400 g potatoes, cut into cubes
3 carrots
1 small bunch root of parsley
3 onions, 2 quartered, 1 whole
3 cloves garlic
1 red chili
2 bay leaves
1 tbsp vinegar
50 g butter
3 tsp sugar
salt and black pepper to taste
2½ litres water
corn oil

garnish
sour cream

borshch

1 Bring to boil 2.5 litres of water, add one carrot, two onions, bay leaves and veal meat. Simmer to make the veal broth, about 1 – 2 hours. **2** Chop one onion, 2 carrots and root of parsley into little pieces. Fry this mixture in a little corn oil till it turns golden in colour. **3** Mix the fried vegetables with the red beet root. Add the vinegar, sugar, chili, salt and pepper. Add about ½ cup of the broth, the butter and stew for about 40 minutes. **4** Blend tomatoes and garlic into a paste. **5** Put the potatoes into the broth and boil for 15 minutes. **6** Add stewed mixture to the cabbage and boil for 10 minutes more. **7** Add the tomato-garlic paste and let stand at a warm place for half an hour. **8** Serve *borshch* in deep plates with a dollop of sour cream on top.

paskha (russian easter dessert)

Paskha means 'Easter' in Russian, and this is a traditional dessert served during the holiday. It is decorated with the Orthodox cross, and the letters 'XB' which are the initials of the Russian words for 'Christ is risen'. The *paskha* is usually taken to the church to be blessed before it is served after the Easter Day dinner.

1½ kg curd pot cheese
½ cup candied, chopped
   fruits and peels, plus
   ½ cup candied fruits
   and peels for garnish
1 tsp vanilla extract
1 cup unsalted butter,
   softened
1 cup heavy cream
4 egg yolks
1 cup sugar
½ cup blanched almonds,
   finely chopped
ice cubes

1 Drain the pot cheese of its moisture by setting it in a colander, covering it with a kitchen towel and weighing it down with a heavy pot. Let the cheese drain for 3 hours. **2** Meanwhile, stir the candied fruits and the vanilla together. Let this mixture stand for one hour. **3** With the back of a wooden spoon, rub the cheese through a fine sieve set over a large bowl. Beat the softened butter thoroughly into the cheese and set aside. **4** Over high heat, scald the cream in a heavy saucepan by heating it until small bubbles form around the edges. Set aside. **5** In a mixing bowl, beat the egg yolks and sugar together for about 10 minutes. While beating, slowly add the hot cream in a thin stream. Pour the mixture into the pan. **6** Stir constantly over low heat until the mixture thickens into a custard-like consistency. Do not allow it to boil. **7** Remove the custard from the heat, stir in the candied fruits and set the pan in a large bowl partially filled with ice cubes covered with water. Stir the custard constantly until it is completely cool, and then mix it gently but thoroughly into the cheese. **8** Stir in the chopped almonds. **9** Set a 2-quart *paskha* form (or a 2-quart clay flowerpot with an opening in the bottom) in a deep plate, and double-line it with dampened cheesecloth cut long enough so that it overhands the rim of the form by 5-cm. **10** Pour in the batter, and fold the ends of the cloth lightly over the top. **11** Set a 1 kg weight directly on top of the cloth and chill *paskha* in a refrigerator overnight. **12** Unwrap the cloth from the top, invert a flat serving plate on top of the pot and grasping the two firmly together, turn them over. The *paskha* will slide out easily. Gently peel off the cloth and decorate the top and sides, as you like. **13** Serves between 12 – 16.

Recipes courtesy of the Embassy of the Russian Federation, Singapore.

chicken kiev

1 Dip bread into milk, then squeeze dry. **2** Mix it together with the minced chicken. Portion the chicken mixture into egg-sized pieces. **3** Roll these pieces out, put a teaspoon of butter on each, and then roll it into a cutlet in the shape of a low cone. **4** Dip the cutlet into the beaten egg, then dredge over breadcrumbs. **5** Heat oil in a saucepan, then fry the cutlet till cooked and golden brown on the outside. Season with salt to taste.

1 chicken, skinned,
   de-boned and minced
300 g butter
150 – 200 g white bread
2 eggs, beaten
milk for dipping
breadcrumbs for coating

balkans

The recent atrocities in the Balkans have prevented visitors from visiting this historically rich land at the junction between Europe and Asia. But now that the dust has somewhat settled, it is very likely that any ethnic cleansing has not rid the region from its culinary traditions.

The influences of Greece, Hungary and Turkey are most discernible in the cuisine of the Balkans. The ubiquitous *burek* (cheese and meat pie) probably unites these countries more than any political treaty as it is eaten throughout the region with equal familiarity. In the South, Albania's palate is heavily lined with Turkish delights. *Shish kebabs*, *romsteak* (minced meat patties) and *qofte* (meat balls) all indicate a strong influence from the Turks. Like most of Europe, lunch is a main affair featuring dishes like *conlek* (meat and onion stew), *rosto me salce kosi* (roast beef with sour cream) and possibly *tave kosi* (mutton with yoghurt). Similarly, in Macedonia, Turkish-style grilled meats are perennial favourites. The exceptions being Macedonian *gravce na tavce* (beans in a skillet) and the fresh trout from the icy cold Lake Ohrid. An Eastern strain is also evident in the food of Bosnia-Hercegovna where *bosanski lonac* (cabbage and meat stew), *baklava* (Turkish pastry), and various grilled meats tend to be the order of the day. Here, *pida* (layered pie of cheese and meat), *sirnica* (cheese pie) and *zeljanica* (spinach pie) point to an iota of Greek influence.

There is little doubt that Yugoslavians love their meat, in any form – stuffed, grilled, in sausages or as *rissoles*. In Montenegro, they throw cholesterol caution to the wind by eating meat with cream and cheese. Croatians share this love for heavy food as is manifested by their love of *piroska*, a cheese doughnut from Zagreb. But Croatia's Adriatic coastline also offers wonderful seafood like *prstaci* (shellfish) and *brodet* (mixed fish stew with rice).

Being the northern-most Balkan country, Slovenia's food possesses of an alpine accent with *klobasa* (sausage), *dunajski zrezek* (*wiener schnitzel*) and *zavitek* (strudel) having an Austrian air. *Rizota* (risotto) and *zlikrofi* (a kind of *ravioli*) have Italian accents and *golaz* (*goulash*) and *paprikas* (chicken or beef stew) are probably Hungarian by origin. Otherwise, cheese dumplings like *strukli* and the Balkan *burek* are stalwart standbys.

The beautifully fertile landform throughout the Balkans is the source of some interesting wines produced in the region. Slovenia and Yugoslavia both produce some notable ones. For more local flavour, *zganje* (Slovenian brandy), *rakija* (Yugoslavian fruit brandy), and *uzo* (Albanian aniseed-flavoured liqueur) often pack enough punch to go with any meal.

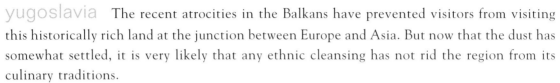

pisana pecenica stubica
(pork tenderloin stubica style)

1 Wash and dry the meat. Wash the prunes and replace the stones with a speck of butter. Seal the prunes. 2 Make a cut through the centre of the meat and stuff the pocket with prunes. 3 Sprinkle with salt and pepper and sauté well in hot oil in a skillet. 4 Add the remaining prunes, cut into thin strips and the *vegeta* into the skillet. Simmer over gentle heat. 5 Add the wine mixed with a little water as necessary. 6 When the meat softens, add the *smetana* and fresh cream. 7 Just before the meat is done, add the *slivovica*. 8 To serve, cut the meat into slices and arrange on a warmed plate. Pour the roasting juices over the meat, sprinkle with parsley and serve with flat noodles or rice. 9 Serves 8 – 10.

5 pork tenderloins
  (about 200 g each)
500 g prunes
1/3 cup oil
80 g butter
3/4 cup *smetana* (a type
  of Croatian cream made
  from skim milk)
1 1/4 cups fresh cream
1 cup white wine
1/4 cup *sljivovica*
  (a Croatian alcoholic drink
  made from plum)
1 tbsp parsley, chopped
2 tbsp *vegeta* (a Croatian
  mixture of dried spices)
salt and pepper

gravche-travce (pan-fried beans)

This is the most famous traditional Macedonian dish. Geographically, it originates from the western part of Macedonia where the particular bean grown is called *tetoec*. This rare white bean is named after the city that is famous for it, Tetovo.

1 Wash the beans and soak in water overnight. 2 The next day, drain the beans, cover with fresh water and bring to a boil. Drain and put in fresh hot water to cover. 3 Add the capsicum and half the chopped onion. Cook until the beans are soft but hold their shape. 4 In another bowl, fry the rest of the chopped onion with a dash of paprika in oil and add this to the beans. 5 Put everything into a oven-proof saucepan and sprinkle with parsley, mint, pepper and salt to taste. 6 Put the pan in an oven heated to about 150 degrees Celcius for about 20 minutes. Be careful not to let the beans dry out. 7 Serve with sausages, ribs, or as is.

500 g white beans
1 onion, chopped
1/3 cup cooking oil
2 – 3 pieces of dry
  red capsicum
dash of paprika
pepper and salt
parsley
mint

janjetina ispod cripnje (lamb baked under a cripnje)

3 kg leg of lamb
2 1/2 kg potatoes, peeled
  and halved lengthwise
500 g onions, sliced
200 ml oil
3 sprigs rosemary
3 bay leaves
salt and pepper to taste

This dish is prepared in a unique Croatian method originating from times long past. Rural communities used to prepare food on an open fire under an inverted bowl covered with coals. The heat-proof bowl is called a *cripnje*, *peka* or a *sace*, depending on which part of the country you are in. Typically, food is placed on a flat, clean stone slab. A *cripnje* is then placed over and hot coals poured over the top of this inverted bowl to cook the food beneath.

1 Wash, dry and cut the lamb into several pieces. Season with salt. 2 Place the meat pieces on the lower part of the *cripnje*. 3 Arrange the potato halves and onion slices around it and add the rosemary and bay leaves. 4 Sprinkle with salt and pepper. 5 Pour the oil over the meat and vegetables and cover with the lid. 6 Heap hot coals over the *cripnje* and bake in an open hearth or baker's oven for 1 1/2 – 2 hours.

pork chops tokay style

Tokay is famous for its wine, in particular, the *aszu*, known to the Hungarians as the "wine of kings, the king of wines". *Aszu* is made from grapes shriveled nearly to raisins when picked in the late fall resulting in a sweet taste that retains its quality for up to 200 years.

1 Beat pork chops lightly, salt, and cover both sides with flour. **2** Place into heated oil and fry till it browns, then arrange them in a casserole. **3** Fry vegetables in remaining juices, season with peppercorn, thyme and bay leaves. **4** Mix in tomato puree. Fry for another 1 – 2 minutes, stirring often, then sprinkle with flour and mix well. **5** Add stock and salt and gently simmer for 35 – 40 minutes. **6** Pour onto meat slices through a fine strainer; add *Tokay aszu* and peeled and pitted grapes. **7** Cover and braise till the meat is tender. **8** To serve, arrange pork chops on a dish, pour the sauce with the grapes and *Tokay aszu* over the meat. **9** Serve with boiled potatoes and parsley in a separate dish. **10** Serves 4.

hungary

Hungarian cuisine accurately reflects the nomadic roots of its people and continuous influence of neighbouring cultures. The quintessential Hungarian dish *gulyás* is not stew, as we know it, but a thick, filling soup of beef and vegetables that originates from a time when the Magyar people were nomadic. These travelers would cook meat over a fire in a cauldron until all the juices had evaporated and the meat had dried. When they wanted a meal all they had to do was to just add water – making them possibly the pioneers of instant cuisine! Even today many Hungarian restaurants still serve *gulyás* in little cauldrons reminiscent of their culinary forefathers.

Paprika, a fragrant spice produced from a range of hot and sweet peppers – supposedly introduced by the Turks – is used extensively as flavouring. It is often added to fresh vegetables, *pörkölt* (thick meat stews), *halászlé* (a spicy fish soup) and *gulyás*, and is utilised to best advantage in the popular *töltött kaposzta* (stuffed cabbage) made of dumplings of minced pork and smoked meats. It is a dish that gets even more delicious with time, hence the Hungarian saying "love isn't like stuffed cabbage because love can't be reheated". Hungarians are enthusiastic consumers of meat, especially pork and beef. But fresh water fish harvested from Hungary's many lakes and rivers are also widely eaten. *Fogas* (pike) is typical and goes particularly well with dumplings braised in a creamy dill sauce. It is even better with a chilled glass of *sauvignon blanc* from Hungary's fast growing wine regions. Hungary has some 20 wine growing areas with the best whites coming from the areas around Lake Balaton in the west and the most distinctive reds from Villány and Szekszárd in the south. Fruit brandies or *pálinka* are popular aperitifs made from cherries, apricots, pears and other fruits – most distinctive of which is the black bitter liqueur called *unicum*. Hungary has managed to embrace many external culinary influences without losing its own character, making its cuisine one of the most exciting and colourful in the world.

600 g pork chops, 4 pieces
15 g salt
50 g flour
¼ cup oil
100 g carrots
100 g parsley root
50 g onions
5 g garlic
2 g peppercorns
1 g thyme
2 bay leaves
30 g concentrated tomato puree
2 cups stock
¾ cup *Tokay aszu* (a wine
  grown in the Tokay region
  of Hungary)
250 g grapes, peeled and pitted

leaven
100 g rye whole meal
½ litre warm water
3 cloves garlic

soup
2 carrots
1 leek
1 bunch parsley
100 g smoked bacon, sliced
200 g white pork sausage
1 ½ litres water
¼ litre leaven for soup
800 g potatoes, boiled and
    mashed with a little butter
2 cloves garlic
4 peppercorns
2 laurel leaves
3 *pimientos*
2 tbsp cream
salt and pepper to taste
lard for frying

zur

leaven: 1 Put the rye whole meal, warm water and garlic into a stoneware pot or glass jar. **2** Mix and cover with a cloth. Keep for a minimum of 5 days in warm temperature. **soup: 3** In a small pan, heat a little lard and fry the sliced smoked bacon. Cook over low heat for 3 minutes, stirring frequently. **4** In a large 3-litre pot, put in the water, vegetables, garlic, peppercorns, laurel leaves, *pimientos* and boil for about 30 minutes. **5** Use a strainer to remove the vegetables. Add the leaven to the soup. Mix well and cook gently for 10 minutes. **6** Add sliced white pork sausages and boil for another 10 minutes. Add the cream. **7** To serve, put the vegetables and potatoes onto a deep plate and spoon soup over it. **8** Top with sautéed smoked bacon together with the lard.

poland

The Poles have a cuisine that is largely unexplored. There is no clear definition of what is true Polish food because it has assimilated the influences of the cuisines of Italy, Russia, Germany, Austria and France. Today, what is deemed as *kuchnia polska* (genuine Polish cuisine) is actually an interesting blend of hearty peasant dishes and more elegant gourmet fare, served with flair and generous hospitality.

The overall taste of Polish food is more inclined towards the tart and tangy. It is a middle-of-the-road European cuisine, which has wide appeal. There is extensive use of honey, raisins, poppy seeds, cloves, nutmeg, ginger, cinnamon, pepper, caraway and saffron. These key ingredients are found in signature dishes like *barszcz* and *zur* (tart soups made with beet-sour, rye-sour or even pickle juice), *rosol* (meat broth with barley) and boiled beef with horseradish. Other piquant favourites include *hussar* beef roast stuffed with onions, *kielbasa* stewed with *sauerkraut*, *kiszka* (goat, blood and variety-meat sausage) and braised goose in rich and fragrant black sauce.

Although Polish food today still retains its essence and character, it is somewhat more refined in presentation, a trait adopted from the French. The Poles are renowned for their hospitality as they take pleasure in bending over backwards to extend the warmest of welcomes to their visitors. This trait is well characterised by their generous and delectable cookery.

103

armenia.azerbaijan.georgia

The countries that make up the Caucasus – Armenia, Azerbaijan and Georgia – share a hybrid commonality that bridges the East and West. This is often manifested in the interesting food that has evolved from this intermingling of people. As is always the case, arresting uniqueness in their cuisines is cause for culinary distinction.

Armenian food is simple and subtly flavoured. Lamb is the staple meat and their specialty of *kashlama* (boiled lamb) is a particular favourite. Other signature dishes include *topig* (made of ground *garbanzo* peas, onions and mashed potatoes), *sudjuk* (a spicy sausage), *basturma* (dried spicy meat), and *keufteh* (stuffed wheat and meatballs) – a dish usually accompanied by *tan* (a yoghurt drink).

The tri-partite influence of Islam, the Turks, and Russia is reflected in the cuisine of Azerbaijan. Their national foods are centred on meat, especially lamb, beef, mutton and poultry, and often accompanied by beets, cabbage, eggplants and spinach. Many dishes are richly spiced with saffron, fennel, coriander, mint and parsley. And *pilaf* (rice fried with meat, fish and vegetables) shows up often at the dining table, accompanied by soup and black tea.

Georgia occupies the central and eastern parts of the Caucasus. Located at the junction of Europe and Asia, the Georgians possess a diverse and moderate culture that has evolved over thousands of years. Georgian food is especially noted for its wide use of all types of meat, fish, cheeses, pickles and piquant seasonings. Key ingredients in their cookery include herbs, garlic, vinegar, red pepper, pomegranate grains and barberries. Typical Georgian food includes *khachapuri* (a thin pie filled with mildly salted cheese), *khinkali* (strongly peppered mutton dumplings), mouth-watering sturgeon on a spit and sauce, *chakapuli* (young lamb in a sourish sauce of damson, herbs and onion) and *khashi* (a beef broth seasoned with garlic). Another favourite dish in the Caucasus is *mcvadi* (skewered meats), which, depending on the season, may be made with pork or mutton.

lentil and bulgur cakes

1 Combine lentils, water and salt in heavy saucepan. Bring to boil, then lower heat and simmer until lentils are tender, about 20 minutes. Add more hot water if needed. **2** Stir in ½ cup butter and *bulgur*. Simmer 2 – 3 minutes. Remove from heat and cover. Set aside for 15 minutes. **3** In a heavy skillet, melt the remaining butter over moderate heat. Sauté onions in the skillet until golden brown. **4** In large mixing bowl combine sautéed onions, lentil and *bulgur* mixture. **5** Dipping hands occasionally into bowl of warm water, knead mixture until well blended. **6** Add 3 tbsp sweet pepper, 3 tbsp green onions, 3 tbsp parsley and 3 tbsp mint to mixture and mix well. Adjust seasonings to taste. **7** Form mixture into ½ patties. Arrange on a serving dish, sprinkle with reserved sweet pepper, green onions, parsley and mint. **8** Season to taste with *paprika* before serving.

1 cup dried lentils
3 cups water
salt to taste
¾ cup butter
¾ cup bulgur, fine grade
1 onion, finely chopped
¼ cup green or sweet red
  pepper, finely chopped
¼ cup green onions,
  finely chopped
¼ cup parsley,
  finely chopped
¼ cup fresh mint,
  finely chopped
paprika to taste

½ tsp coriander seed
½ tsp cardamom seed
½ tsp ground cinnamon
1 tsp cumin seed
1 clove
2 tbsp vegetable oil
1 kg lamb, cut into 5-cm chunks
1 kg onion, peeled and minced
4 garlic cloves,
  peeled and minced
2 carrots, peeled and
  cut into pieces
1 celery root, peeled and
  cut into pieces
4 tomatoes, peeled, cored,
  and cut into pieces
1 acorn squash, peeled and
  cut into pieces
8 cups chicken broth
1 2½-kg pumpkin, cleaned
1 cup basmati rice, uncooked
½ tsp salt
1 tsp black pepper, freshly ground
¼ cup coriander leaves, minced
¾ cup parsley leaves, minced

armenian pumpkin stew

1 Combine coriander, cardamom, cinnamon, cumin and clove in a spice mill or coffee grinder. Grind until smooth and set aside. **2** Heat 1 tbsp of oil in large, heavy-bottom saucepan and sprinkle spice mixture over it. **3** Sear the lamb in this mixture over medium heat until lightly browned. Remove the lamb from the pan and set aside. **4** Sauté the onion and garlic in the pan for about 5 minutes. Add the carrots, celery root, tomatoes and acorn squash. Add the broth. **5** Return lamb to the pan. Partly cover and gently simmer until the meat is tender, about 2 hours. Season with salt and pepper. **6** While the lamb is cooking, preheat the oven to 175 degrees Celsius. **7** Place the pumpkin on a baking sheet. Brush the outside with the remaining oil. Bake until tender, about 1 hour. **8** Cook the rice and set aside. **9** To serve, place the pumpkin in a serving dish and fill it with the lamb stew. Garnish with coriander and parsley and serve with the rice. **10** Serves 4.

turkey

Truly the land where East meets West. At the Bosphorus Strait, Asia shakes hands with the European Mediterranean, bringing a marriage of cultures and, in no lesser extent, foods from both continents. Furthermore, with geographical assets equal to that found in Europe, Africa and Asia, Turkey is itself a giant in food production – it is one of seven countries in the world that produces more than enough for local consumption. It goes without saying that Turkish food reflects the diversity of the land and all its regional variations.

In the rugged highlands of the Eastern region, livestock farming is prevalent. Dairy products, meat and cereals are commonly made into dishes like yoghurt soup and meatballs, sustenance enough to ward off those long cold winters. Moving westwards, the country takes on a more agricultural slant where wheat fields and orchards surround the city of Konya, capital of the ancient Seljuk Empire. Here, regional specialties like *kebabs*, *börek* (layered pastry), and *helva* (a desert made of semolina flour cooked in butter, in which milk and sugar are added till all is absorbed into a cake-like pastry) date back to the early 13th century.

Being surrounded by four seas – the Aegean, Mediterranean, Black and Marmara – the coastal regions are a treasure trove of seafood. Among the Turks, *hamsi*, a type of anchovy, assumes princely status and is used to make many different dishes, for e.g. *hamsi pilaf*, *hamsi borek* and even *hamsi* dessert.

Eating in Turkey is a communal obligation and dining alone is unheard of. Family and friends often gather on the floor, picking food from a *sini* (round metal tray) sitting atop a small stool. The process often begins with a warm-up of sorts. Tiny dishes of *mete* (similar to the *meze* of North Africa) are the perfect accompaniment to the local gossip and a round of *raki*, the anise-flavoured national drink of the Turks (also called 'lion's milk'). The meal proper commonly consists of either grilled meats like *kebabs* or *köfte* (prepared ground meat) or seafood accompanied by vegetables. Turkish preparations are purist in essence, spices and herbs are used sparingly allowing the natural flavours of the produce or meat to come through. Customarily, no meal is complete without some form of carbohydrate. Breads like *ekmek* (white bread) and *pide* (flat bread), or *pilaf* are often integral to the meal. Turkish desserts are far from restricted to the familiar Turkish delights or *baklava* (layered pastry filled with nuts, baked and sweetened with syrup). *Kadayif* (a pastry made from sheet dough) or various kinds of rice puddings (e.g. *sutlac*, *zerde* and *muhallebi*) are just as respectable a way to end a feast together with a punch of black, thick Turkish coffee.

2 kg lamb, cut into chunks
   suitable for stews
4 tbsp butter
3 onions, sliced
1 tbsp tomato paste
1 tbsp flour
6 tomatoes, cut into chunks
1½ litre water
1 tsp thyme
4 cloves garlic
2 bay leaves
1 tsp peppercorns
1 pinch parsley stems
salt to taste

eggplant purée
10 eggplants
juice from 1 lemon
4 tbsp butter
1 tbsp flour
200 g milk, boiled
salt and pepper to taste
1 cup grated *gruyere* cheese

hunkar begendi (sultan's delight with eggplant purée)

1 Melt butter in a saucepan, add the lamb chunks and roast for 8 – 10 minutes. **2** Add sliced onions and tomato paste, fry for two more minutes, then add flour. **3** Place the thyme, garlic, bay leaves, peppercorns and parsley in a small muslin bag to form a *bouquet garni*. **4** Add to the meat with salt and water. Then add the tomato chunks to the meat and cook for about 10 – 15 minutes over low heat. **purée: 5** Pierce eggplants with a fork, then place over an open flame or under a hot broiler in the oven. Cook for half an hour, turning often to prevent burning. Remove from heat, and let cool. **6** Cut eggplants in half and scoop out pulp. Mash pulp with a fork to form a purée and add lemon juice. **7** Melt butter in a saucepan, then add the flour and cook over low heat to form a roux. **8** Add boiled milk, salt and pepper and continue to stir. **9** Mix eggplant in with the milk mixture and add the cheese. Mash with a fork until the whole mixture forms a paste. **10** Pour eggplant purée onto a serving dish, make a hollow in the center of it and place the meat in its hollow. Dish a little of the meat's juice over the dish and serve. **11** Serves 8 – 10.

western
europe

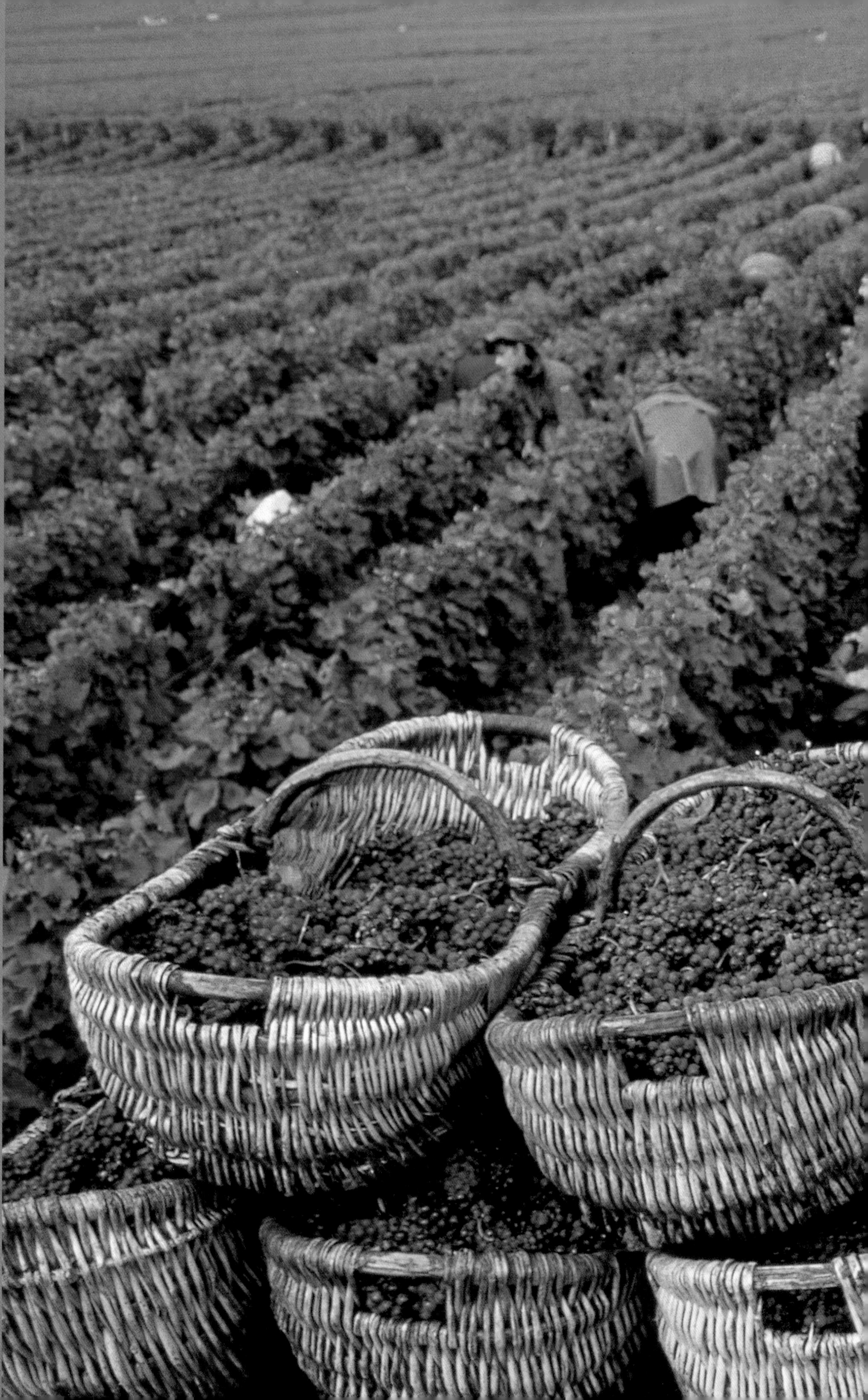

1 ANDORRA 2 AUSTRIA 3 BELGIUM 4 CYPRUS

5 DENMARK 6 FINLAND 7 FRANCE 8 GERMANY

9 UNITED KINGDOM 10 GREECE 11 ICELAND

12 IRELAND 13 ITALY 14 LIECHTENSTEIN

15 LUXEMBOURG 16 MALTA 17 MONACO

18 NETHERLANDS 19 NORWAY 20 PORTUGAL

21 SAN MARINO 22 SPAIN 23 SWEDEN

austria.liechtenstein

Austria's place in the music world has been made eternal by Struass waltzes, his lilting waves of notes flowing like the tide along the river Danube. In the same way as a composer is swayed by all that surrounds him, so too has Austria's many neighbours influenced its food. Roast beef (originally from England), *goulash* (Hungary), *schnitzel* (Italy) are all dishes with foreign origins that are found as everyday fare in Austrian homes as well as on *gasthaus* (simple restaurants serving traditional food) menus.

Foreign influence not withstanding, the different regions of Austria have also made their individual mark on the dining table. For one, Vienna's confectionery and love for coffee have made the Viennese café an international icon. This historic city is also the birthplace of *wiener schnitzel*, the breaded veal chop of worldwide recognition. The *sachertorte*, invented by Franz Sacher and made famous by his son Eduard, has also found its way into any respectable baker's repertoire. Austria shares its border with Italy, Hungary, Yugoslavia, Germany, Switzerland and Czechoslovakia, each imparting an accent on the Austrian culinary spectrum. In the Burgenland region, previously part of Hungary, beans are found in all manner and form in the region's dishes. In the lower Austrian region, an area bordering Bohemia and Moravia, potato and poppy are the predominant crops and are used to make dishes like *skubanki* (fried potato dumplings rolled in poppy seed and covered with powdered sugar and melted butter).

In the northern reaches of Austria, German influence is clearly apparent. Dumplings are the specialty here ranging from *reiberknodel* (grated dumplings) and *griessknodel* (semolina dumplings) to *mehlknodel* (flour dumplings) and *brotknodel* (bread dumplings). Salzburg, Mozart's birthplace, on the other hand, is famous for its beer. Beer soup is an unusual dish from this state and is made by adding butter, egg yolk and cream to boiling beer, and then garnishing with salt, pepper, nutmeg and sugar.

Austrian food is steeped in history and tinged with geographical accents. But the inevitable shifting balance between tradition and innovation has given rise to a slew of chefs who have made headlines around the world for their creative interpretation of classical cuisine. The cuisine of Liechtenstein borrows from its neighbours, Austria being one of them. Cheeses are popular, so are potatoes (in the form of *rostis* – fried shredded potatoes) and *wurst* (sausages). *Kasknopfle*, a traditional dish, is prepared by baking flour and egg dumplings with cheese and topped with sautéed onions. The country also prides itself in its wine, unfortunately, most of it is consumed within its own borders.

³/₄ cup butter
1 cup flour
180 g semi-sweet chocolate
10 egg whites, stiffly beaten
³/₄ cup sugar
2 tbsp apricot jam
8 egg yolks

chocolate icing
1 cup sugar
¹/₃ cup water
200 g semi-sweet chocolate

sachertorte (sacher cake)

1 Beat butter till creamy; melt chocolate, add sugar and chocolate to butter, stir. 2 Add egg yolks one at a time, then add the flour, fold in egg whites till all is well blended. 3 Pour mixture into a well-greased cake tin. Bake in 135 degrees Celsius oven for about 1 hour or till a cake tester comes out clean. Remove and cool. 4 When cooled, cut top off and turn bottom up. Warm the apricot jam and spread over the top. Cover with chocolate icing. For a variation, the cake may be split into two or three layers and filled with apricot jam or whipped cream. **icing: 5** Cook sugar and water. Melt chocolate in the top of a double boiler. Add sugar water gradually to chocolate, stirring constantly until icing coats the spoon. 6 Pour on top of cake when ready.

kasknopfle

200 g flour
1 egg
salt
water to make a stiff dough
cheese, mixture of fat cheese
  (e.g. Swiss) and sour cheese
1 onion, sliced
oil for frying
3 tbsp butter, hot melted
water for boiling

1 Mix the flour and egg. Add enough fresh cold water to form a stiff dough ball. It should not be too dry, or too sticky. 2 Put dough into a sliding cutter fixed with a grater. Push dough through the cutter into boiling salted water. Dumplings formed should be the size of marble. 3 Once the dumplings rise to the top, remove form the boiling water with a slotted spoon. Briefly pour cold water over the dumplings and drain. 4 Place some dumplings into a baking pan, sprinkle the grated cheese mixture over the layer, then repeat until all the dumplings are used up. 5 In a separate frying pan, fry the sliced onions till brown and crispy. 6 Pour butter and fried onions over the dumplings and serve with potato salad, green salad, or even apple sauce.

mussels in beer

1 Rinse the mussels in plenty of water. **2** Melt butter in a pan. Sweat the diced vegetables and herbs for a few moments, and then add beer. Bring to a boil. **3** Put the mussels in the boiling liquid till they open. Add salt, pepper and nutmeg to taste. **4** Take the mussels out of the liquid and shell them, removing their beards. **5** Strain the liquid and add a few knobs of butter. **6** Serve the mussels on plates and top them with the sauce. **7** Decorate with the chervil and parsley. **8** Serves 4.

belgium.luxembourg

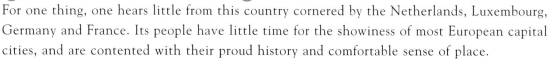

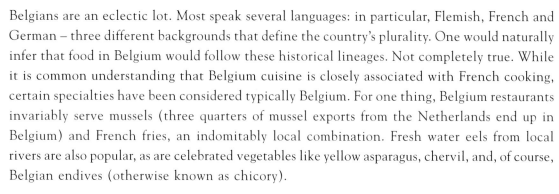

Belgium is like a secret waiting to be discovered. For one thing, one hears little from this country cornered by the Netherlands, Luxembourg, Germany and France. Its people have little time for the showiness of most European capital cities, and are contented with their proud history and comfortable sense of place.

Belgians are an eclectic lot. Most speak several languages: in particular, Flemish, French and German – three different backgrounds that define the country's plurality. One would naturally infer that food in Belgium would follow these historical lineages. Not completely true. While it is common understanding that Belgium cuisine is closely associated with French cooking, certain specialties have been considered typically Belgium. For one thing, Belgium restaurants invariably serve mussels (three quarters of mussel exports from the Netherlands end up in Belgium) and French fries, an indomitably local combination. Fresh water eels from local rivers are also popular, as are celebrated vegetables like yellow asparagus, chervil, and, of course, Belgian endives (otherwise known as chicory).

On the sweeter front, Belgian chocolates are well known for their smooth, rich countenance and are one of Belgium's most successful food export. And the thick, light and fluffy Belgian waffles (eaten with powdered sugar, butter, whipped cream, or all of the above) are like nothing found west of Flanders.

If there is one thing the Belgians are most noted for, it is beer. There are reportedly more than 300 different labels of beer in Belgium. They range from micro-breweries that brew a single flavour to foreign-owned conglomerates producing for the international market. Walk into any pub and one is likely to be recommended a particular label from the backroom or a nearby monastery.

1 kg mussels
3 sticks celery, diced
1 carrot, diced
1 onion, diced
1 sprig thyme
1 bunch chervil
1 bunch parsley
1 bottle *pilsner* (a pale beer)
salt, pepper and nutmeg to taste

Despite being a small country, Belgium does have its share of regional culinary distinctions. Along the short coastline of the Northwest, a vibrant fishing industry supports a diet of seafood. And in the southern region of Ardennes, the hilly woodlands are plum hunting grounds for game like venison, pheasant, rabbit and wild boar – delicacies all. The country's size has little bearing on the people's zest for life. The fervor placed on food matches any culinary-inclined culture in the world. Belgium is a nation of individuals with the capacity to celebrate the pleasure of food and drink in their own understated way.

The cuisine of Luxembourg, like the culture itself, takes a cue from its neighbouring countries. The food here is much like that of Belgium's Wallonia region. Pork, fish and game meats are popular, and German influence is evident in the form of *sauerkraut* and liver dumplings.

600 g minced beef
2 large yellow onions
150 g butter for frying
salt and pepper to taste

potatoes
8 – 10 potatoes
1 tsp salt

sauce
butter left over from
  frying steaks
1 tsp balsamic vinegar
1 cup water
1 tbsp ketchup
1 tsp worcestershire sauce
2 tsp cornstarch
salt and pepper to taste

denmark

Food in Denmark is very much like the people of the country – straightforward, honest and elegant in its simplicity. The Danish – the pastry that has adopted the country's namesake – is representative of this characteristic. Though humble in appearance, the essence is in its substance. Buttery velvet, a melt in your mouth experience that is inevitably memorable and addictive.

With a population of less than 6 million, Denmark is unsurprisingly one of the largest per capita producers of food products in the world. Pick up a can of ham, pork shoulder or sausage in any grocery store and more often than not, it has come from this country. The popularity of processed pork products belies its geographical landform. Being surrounded by water, the Danish fishing ports of Esbjerg, Hanstholm, Hirtschals and Skagen have spurned a thriving fishing industry producing cod, herring, salmon, trout, eels, caviar, and a host of other seafood items, for home consumption as well as export.

People here eat as simply as a lunch of chunky bread topped with pieces of cold meat and cheese (known as *smorrebord*), or as elaborately as at a traditional buffet called a *smorgasbord* – otherwise known as *kolde bord*, or 'cold table', in Danish. In this gastronomical free-for-all, one typically finds fish, meat, poultry, vegetables (prepared in a grand variety of ways) as well as an exhaustive rendition of breads, pastries and desserts.

The Christmas season is traditionally the time of year that brings the best out of Danish appetites. Roast geese and duck find their way onto family tables accompanied by an ensemble of red cabbage, roasted potatoes and the ubiquitous thick brown sauce. Rice pudding (called *ris a l'amande*) topped with cherry sauce is a typical way to end the seasonal meal.

Like any other time of year, the libation of choice is an ice cold Carlsberg, the predominant brand of beer that has achieved international repute. Otherwise, a quick shot of Danish *schnapps* (a *vodka*-like alcohol) will surely add spark to any occasion.

danish mince beef steaks with fried onions, boiled potatoes and sauce

1 Wash potatoes, place them in a pot and cover with water. Add the salt and boil for about half an hour over medium heat. When cooked, drain the potatoes and peel off the skin. Cover until time to serve. **2** Shape minced beef into about 8 patties (about 1 cm in height). Season with salt and pepper. **3** Heat some butter in a pan till golden brown, add patties and fry over medium heat for about 3 minutes on each side. Place patties on a tray and cover before serving. **sauce: 4** Combine the leftover butter from frying the beef with the balsamic vinegar. Add the water, ketchup and Worcestershire sauce. Let boil for about 2 minutes before seasoning with salt and pepper. **5** Thicken the sauce by dissolving the cornstarch in a little water, then pouring the mixture into the sauce. Pour sauce into a sauce pan and cover before serving. **fried onions: 6** Peel the onions and slice thinly. **7** Heat the rest of the butter in a pan till golden brown, add the onion slices and stir fry till the onion is soft and golden brown. Season with a little salt and pepper. **8** To combine the dish, place onion on top of each beef steak and serve with potatoes and sauce.

finland

Food from Finland is food from nature's own garden. The basic elements from the Finnish kitchen consist of the treasures of the land and sea: game, fish, mushrooms, wild berries and flowers. These ingredients rely so much on their natural flavour that cooking in this country does not need complicated methods or strong spices.

Food of the Finns comes from an amalgamation of influences from Russia, on the one hand, Scandinavia and Germany on the other, thus creating a certain marriage of Eastern and Western European cooking styles. Nearly two hundred thousand lakes punctuate Finland. Together with numerous rivers and a long coastline, it comes as little wonder that fish, and fishing, is an integral part of the Finnish lifestyle and diet. Perch is the national fish, but salmon, rainbow trout, pike, whitefish and Baltic herring also rank high on the country's offerings.

Despite its Nordic location, Finland is still pretty much an agricultural country. Bread (particularly rye), dairy products and potatoes are still important in local diets. The common, and popular, presence of a smoking box comes in useful in cooking and preserving fish and meat, especially when winter rolls around. Inside the homes, a large oven serves several purposes. During the long cold months, it is not unusual for a household to use the oven for both cooking and heating. Pastries and bread are first baked in the oven, then meat and vegetable stews and casseroles take over – slow cooked for hours to provide a hearty meal, and in the process, comfortable warmth.

Finns have an affinity to nature. Most have summer homes from which they spend the precious warm months picking wild berries and mushrooms. There are ninety different kinds of mushrooms found in Finland, and picking them for commercial use can be a profitable excursion through the beautiful land.

500 g perch fillets
500 g salmon, sliced finely
600 g fresh spinach
water
1 medium onion, chopped
100 g butter
200 g fresh mushrooms, sliced
salt, pepper, nutmeg
3 egg whites
400 g thick cream

salmon and perch tart

1 Wash, and then blanch spinach with boiling water for 2 minutes. Cool in cold water and squeeze the water out thoroughly. **2** Cook chopped onions in 80 g of the butter. Add the mushrooms and fry until the liquid has evaporated. Add the spinach and heat well; season with salt, pepper and nutmeg. Set aside to cool. **3** Cut perch into cubes, season with salt, pepper and nutmeg. Put in a cold place for 10 minutes. **4** Purée the perch cubes in a food processor, add the egg whites one by one. Finally, pour in the cream. Season to taste. **5** Butter a 24 – 26 cm diameter cake tin with the remaining butter. **6** Spread the spinach mixture evenly over the base of the tin, pressing it down. Pipe half the perch mixture over the spinach and smoothen. **7** Place all the salmon slices evenly on the mixture and season with salt and pepper. **8** Pipe the rest of the perch mixture over the salmon and smoothen. **9** Heat oven to 170 degrees Celsius. Cover the cake tin with buttered aluminum foil. Place the tin in a deep baking dish and pour in water at 70 degrees Celsius to a depth of 3 cm. Bake in this *bain marie* for 50 – 60 minutes. **10** When the tart is ready, loosen its sides with a knife and turn out on a serving dish. **11** Serve with fresh tomatoes, white wine or shrimp sauce.

france

Just as artists have always been attracted to the South of France for it's unusual quality of light, food connoisseurs flock the nation's kitchens for the exceptional food. The multitude of restaurants and cafés all over France showcases the diversity and artistry of the French chef. It was the French revolution that brought fine French cuisine to the people. Before the revolution, the best chefs served only in the palaces preparing feasts and banquets, but after the toppling of the French monarchy these chefs found themselves out of a job ... bringing on the advent of the full service restaurant.

An essential feature of fine French cuisine is the use of the finest ingredients. On top of that, diversity in French food is manifested in a myriad of cooking styles. Distinguishing them can be bewildering. *Alsacienne* cuisine originating from the Alsace region bordering Germany often makes use of numerous garnishes such as *liver paté, sauerkraut* or sausages. *Consummé a l'alsacienne* (chicken *consummé* simmered with *sauerkraut* and *strasborg* sausages) is typical of this region. Provence in the Southeast of France boasts warm weather and the sun-kissed beaches of the French Riviera. Distinctly Mediterranean, Provençial cuisine makes more use of olive oil, garlic and spices than many other regions that use butter to enrich most dishes. Considered by many to be the gastronomic capital of France, Lyon is home to the simple but delicious *coq au vin*, a dish of browned chicken joints with salt pork and shallots braised with a whole bottle of strong dry *Beaujolais* and liberally enriched in butter. This abundance of cooking styles is matched by the multitude of wines available, each carefully designed over generations to reflect the character of the local cuisine.

While wines from Australia, Chile and California have become common on the table, a bottle of French wine carries a distinction all its own. From the sharp crisp *Alsacienne Rieslings* and the sparkling champagnes of the North, to the rich fragrant *côte de Provence* and *tannic Corbières* of the South, the wines of France invoke a sense of place for the food of the country, marking itself outstandingly amongst the world's most revered cuisines.

LA METHODE

In French cooking, the road from produce to plate is lined with many a detour. The number of cooking methods is as vast as imagination itself. It is therefore no easy task trying to decipher the nature of a French dish from its name on a menu, even if you speak the language.

The following list is just the tip of the proverbial iceberg of classic French food preparations. However, it is as good as any a place to start.

* *A l'Antillaise* – fish preparation with thick vegetable sauce and tomato, often served with rice
* *A l'Ardennaise* – game dishes prepared with juniper (in the form of spirits or berries)
* *A l'Anglaise* – vegetables cooked in water and served with melted butter; meat or poultry cooked in white stock; fish or meat coated with breadcrumbs and sautéed or fried
* *A la Benedictine* – dishes using purée of salt cod and potato
* *A la Chartres* – method of cooking egg and meat using tarragon
* *A la Dauphine* – method of preparing vegetables where the vegetables are mashed, added to *choux* pastry and deep-fried
* *A la Florentine* – method of preparation using spinach
* *A la Gauloise* – dishes with cocks' combs and kidneys

* *A la Languedocienne* – dishes that include tomatoes, aubergines, mushrooms, together or separately
* *A la Maltaise* – sweet or savoury dishes prepared with oranges
* *A la Marechale* – small cuts of meats coated with breadcrumbs and sautéed
* *A La Mariniere* – seafood cooked in white wine with onions and shallots
* *A La Printaniere* – dishes garnished with mixture of vegetables tossed in butter
* *A La Sicilienne* – small pieces of fried meat garnished with stuffed tomatoes, rice timbales and potato croquettes
* *A La Tahitienne* – marinated raw fillet of fish
* *A La Toscane* – dishes prepared with Parmesan cheese and ham

le cassoulet

160 dry haricot beans
2 cloves garlic, bruised
1 onion
2 carrots, peeled and cut into cubes
a small bunch of thyme, or parsley
1 duck, legs and wings removed and reserved
1 pork knuckle
500 g pork top ribs
200 g bacon, about 4 strips
4 sausages
pepper
oil

This is a specialty from Southwest France.

1 Steep the dry haricot beans in fresh water for about 12 hours. Drain and set aside. **2** Soak the pork knuckle in water, if salted, for about an hour. Drain the pork knuckle, dry it, then fry it slightly without any spices except pepper. **3** Stew the duck with a little oil till tender. Drain and set aside the fat. **4** In a deep pan, pour in the haricot beans, the garlic cloves, carrots, the whole onion, the herbs, pork top ribs, pork knuckle and the bacon. Add the duck grease and enough water to cover all the ingredients. Bring to a boil and simmer for 1½ hours, uncovered. **5** Meanwhile, fry the sausages. **6** Pour the stew and the sausages in an ovenproof dish. Add the duck legs and wings, and some pepper grains. Cover with more water if the stew has dried out. **7** Place in a 140 degrees Celsius oven and cook for 2½ hours. A crust will form on the top from time to time. Break it and stir lightly, no more than 5 – 7 times. **8** Grill in the oven for another 15 minutes before serving. **9** Serves 4.

eisbein mit sauerkraut
(knuckle of pork with sauerkraut)

1 Rinse the pork knuckle in cold water, then place in the salted water. Bring to a boil and simmer for 1¹⁄₂ hours. **2** Put the *sauerkraut* into the pot, then the onion, cloves and the bay leaf. **3** Bring to a boil and simmer for another hour. **4** Wash, peel, rinse, and grate the potato and add to the pot. **5** Bring briefly to a the boil and simmer till the mixture becomes thick and creamy. **6** Season with sugar, salt and pepper. **7** Serve with mashed potatoes.

1¹⁄₂ kg pork knuckle
1 cup salted water
750 g *sauerkraut*
1 medium onion
1 bay leaf
3 cloves
1 medium potato
sugar, salt and freshly
   ground pepper to taste

germany

Germany is a beautiful country of delightful contrasts – sea and mountains, bleak moorlands and dense forests, busy cities and rural farmland. It is because their geography spans from the cool rainy North to the almost Mediterranean Rhine Valley in the South that their cuisine ranges from rustic and hearty fare to haute cuisine in the cosmopolitan areas.

Things found on the dining table differ greatly depending on which part of the country one is in. In Hamburg, eel soup is commonplace, whereas in Baden-Wurttenberg, one would find excellent asparagus as the main ingredient in many dishes. In Swabia, *maultaschen* (a type of *ravioli*) and *spatzle* (tiny flour dumplings) are the norm. In Brandenburg Marches, the signature dish is roast goose with different types of vegetables. One will find the famous *katenschinken* (a strongly flavoured streaky ham) in East Holstein. Cologne and Wolfenbuttel are popular for the famous Westphalian ham, *braunschweiger mettwurst* (a local Brunswick sausage), pumpernickel bread and Rhineland black rye bread. The Rhineland is also known for its top quality wines, from *Pinot Noir*, *Pinot Gris* and *Pinot Blanc*, to full-bodied *Rieslings*. One common denominator in all regions, however, is the staple of potatoes. These are served simply boiled, baked, pan-fried or made into pancakes.

Certain foods are instantly associated with Germany outside of the country. Famous German culinary inventions that have been well-received include *sauerkraut* (strips of salted and fermented white cabbage), sausages, *sauerbraten* (game or beef pickled in vinegar), *stollen* (a Christmas dough cake with marzipan and candied fruit), *blackforest cake* (a chocolate cake filled with sour cherries, laced with *kirsch* and topped with cream), German beer and *schnapps* (an after-dinner liqueur made from distilled barley, rye or wheat).

In a nutshell, there is no one dish that fully represents Germany. Instead, their 'patchwork-style' cuisine reflects their history, now woven into a tapestry of a coherent, yet diverse nation.

united kingdom

Food in the UK is like the land and people that pervade in this kingdom by the sea, united by a common thread, yet distinct in their many subtleties. As one travels from the warm Cornwall coast to the frigid waters of the Scottish north, the variation in geography, language and culture is reflected in the cuisine of the British.

In England, a day is often jump-started with a hearty breakfast made up of egg, bacon, sausage, grilled mushrooms and tomato with toast, washed down with fragrant tea or coffee. Kippers – herrings that have been split, gutted, salted and smoked – are always a unique alternative as well. Lunch may be fish and chips, beef wellington (fillet steak wrapped in puff pastry with mushroom and onion filling, served with port wine sauce), cornish pasty (a pastry with meat filling on one end and jam filling on the other), shepherd's pie (minced lamb with potato topping) or steak and kidney pudding (a suet pudding with steak and kidneys). Typical English desserts include baked custard, served with stewed fruit; summer pudding (made with raspberries, blueberries and blackberries) and Dorset apple cake (a cake containing apples and currants). Of course, classic scones, served with clotted cream and strawberry jam, and buttered cucumber sandwiches invariably accompanied by tea has made the mid-afternoon snack an institution.

Arguably, at least in the culinary sense, the Scots are most noted for *haggis*, a tasty, rich and spicy concoction of lamb's offal mixed with suet, onions, herbs and spices packed into a sheep's stomach. This is usually eaten with mashed potatoes, or mashed swede or turnips. Other popular dishes include herring (served fried, grilled, stuffed or baked with oatmeal) and *cock-a-leekie*, a broth made with roasted chicken or game birds, potatoes, leeks, pork sausages and breakfast prunes. A typical Scottish pudding is *cranachan*, toasted oatmeal steeped in whiskey and folded into whipped cream flavoured with fresh raspberries. *Atholl brose*, a sweet yet nutty potent drink, or the indigenous dark beer served at room temperature are popular alcoholic beverages. And of course, Scotch whiskey is legendary.

Signature Welsh dishes include *bara lawr* (laver bread), a tasty seaweed and oatmeal cake, often fried with a traditional breakfast of pork sausages, egg and bacon; *cawl* (a chunky mutton and vegetable broth), usually eaten with bread and *caws aberteifi* (a cheese made in Cardigan); and their native lamb, served minted or with thyme.

The national favourites in Northern Ireland would include the quintessential Irish stew, a mutton or lamb stew cooked with carrots, potatoes, onions, parsley and thyme; *dublin coddle* (a semi-thick stew made with sausages, bacon, onions and potatoes), *colcannon* (a traditional meatless stew of potatoes, cabbage and onions) and soda bread, a tasty, grainy and moist cake-like bread. These would be accompanied by world-renowned Guinness stout or Irish coffee (made with whiskey, brown sugar, hot black coffee and cream) or just Irish cream (a mixture of dairy cream with coffee or chocolate).

Although the traditional foods of the U.K. form an indelible part of British history and culture, over the last few years New British food has carved out an identity by combining classical methods with new, fresh ideas from different parts of the world.

750 g potatoes
750 g lamb, middle of the neck cut
1 large onion, sliced
mixed herbs
salt and pepper to taste
½ cup stock

lancashire hot pot

This simple dish is a local favourite in the North of England. It was originally made with cheap ingredients to warm up the impoverished miners after a hard day's work in the coal mines.

1 Peel and slice the potatoes, then arrange them in a layer at the bottom of a casserole dish. **2** Slice the meat into pieces and place on top of the potatoes. **3** Add the sliced onion. Repeat steps 1 – 3 and finish by topping with a layer of potatoes. **4** Add the mixed herbs, salt and pepper to the stock, and then pour over the potatoes. Cover with a lid or aluminum foil. **5** Bake in a moderate oven for 2 hours, but remove the cover over the last 15 minutes. **6** Serves 4 – 6.

WHAT'S IN A NAME

The Queen's English was probably never meant to be this complicated. But where British food is concerned, things aren't always what they seem to be. The following are a sample of some traditional British fare where what you hear isn't necessarily what you get:

* *Spotted Dick* – a kind of steamed raisin pudding served with custard sauce
* *Spotted Dog* – a boiled sweet pudding made with suet and raisins
* *Toad In The Hole* – breakfast of fresh sausages baked in a batter
* *Singing Hinnies* – hotcakes from the isle of Cape Breton in Nova Scotia
* *Bubble and Squeak* – potatoes and cabbage fried with egg
* *Welsh Rarebit* – melted cheese over sliced bread
* *Eton Mess* – traditional snack of strawberries, whipped cream and meringue eaten by parents and pupils of the Eton school during the prize giving in June

dolmas (stuffed grapevine leaves)

1 In a skillet, fry the onions in the olive oil, add parsley, rice, nuts, dill, lemon peel and raisins. **2** Fry till nuts are brown, then pour in 1½ cup of the broth, cover, and simmer for about 15 minutes. **3** Place leaves flat with the vein side facing up. Scoop about 1 tbsp of the filling onto the centre of each leaf. Fold in the sides and roll upwards. **4** Mix 1½ cups broth with ½ cup of olive oil and the lemon juice. **5** Place stuffed grape leaves seam side down in a kettle or dutch oven. After placing *dolmas* in a single layer, pour half of the broth mixture over the leaves. Add the rest of the stuffed grape leaves and then the rest of the mixture. **6** Bring to a boil over moderate heat, reduce heat and simmer for about 45 minutes. **7** Serve warm or at room temperature.

greece

Food in Greece is a child of the land, as well as of a history shared with Macedonia, the Balkans, and in part, Italy. But it is the influence from the ancient Ottoman Empire that has put an indelible stamp on Greek food today. It has provided it with a sophistication from the Middle East manifesting in the use of spices like cumin in meat, the practice of stuffing vegetables, and making savoury pastries. The famed Mediterranean climate and fertile land is the palette from which Greek food is created. Olives and olive oil; lamb; goat's cheese; and excellent wines all characterised what is wonderful about the wholesome, healthy cuisine. Meat is generally featured at a meal, with lamb – braised, in a stew, grilled, or broiled – being a favourite. Meat and vegetables often form a triumphant duo, accented with a touch of lemon, a fruit that the country grows in abundance.

Across the many romantic islands of Greece, the *ouzerie* and *kafeneon* (coffee houses) are fabled – serving *mezedes* (appetisers) with *ouzo* (a local liquor) to while away the lazy afternoons. From the vibrant Aegean Sea, *percha* (sea perch), *scorpena* (scorpion fish), *selaki* (ray) and *barbounia* (red mullet) are treasures harvested for the dining table. Octopus is a specialty – served as *octapodi me kremithia* (stewed in onions) or with rice or pasta as in the *oktapodi pilafi*.

In the Dodecanese and Ionian islands, the influence of the Venetians is palpable. Greeks in this region eat more pasta and cured meats – like the Italians – and use less spices as well. In the mountain region, *spetsofai* (mix of country sausages and green peppers) is typical, and one of the most representative of Greek dishes. *Fasolia gigantes* (beans baked in the oven, or made into soup); *gida vrasti* (boiled goat); *galotiri* (soft goat's cheese with *paprika*); and stews like *hirino me prasa* (pork and leeks) are foods that give satisfying sustenance in the harsh, elevated climate.

250 g grape leaves, blanched
    in boiling water and drained
    (stems removed)
2 tbsp olive oil
1 onion, chopped
3 tbsp fresh parsley, minced
1 cup rice, raw
¼ cup pine nuts
1 tsp dill, chopped
¼ cup raisins, chopped
½ tsp lemon peel, minced
3 cups chicken broth
½ cup olive oil
5 tbsp lemon juice

iceland

Iceland is a country of extremes. Endless days in summer and the reverse in winter typify this country known for its glaciers and geysers. By and large, the cuisine of such a land is hardly expected to be very predictable.

To enjoy the food of Iceland requires a stolid resolve lined with a sense of adventure. Traditional Icelandic dishes might include *hárkarl* (putrefied shark meat, buried in sand and gravel for three to six months to ensure decomposition); *súsaôir hrútspungar* (ram's testicles pickled in whey and pressed into a cake), *sviô* (singed sheep's head with eyes intact, sawn in two and boiled, eaten either fresh or pickled); and *slátur* (sheep leftovers tied up in sheep's stomach and cooked).

However, Iceland also has some less bizarre dishes that are a little more palatable to the uninitiated. The lay visitor to the country would be thankful for *harôfiskur* (haddock air-dried, torn into strips and eaten with butter as a snack); *hangikjöt* (literally 'hung meat' – which is smoked lamb); and broiled *lundi* (puffin) – a little penguin-like bird that tastes like calf's liver. One of the more easily accepted and delectable Icelandic dishes is their dessert called *skyr* – a concoction made of pasteurised skim milk and a bacteria culture used to make sourdough. This low-fat concoction is mixed with sugar, fruit flavours and milk – to give it a creamy yoghurt-like texture – and topped with wild crowberries.

Little alcohol is consumed in Iceland due to the government's prohibitive measures to deter consumption. However, there is one traditional Icelandic brew called *brennivin* (literally 'burnt wine'), a sort of *schnapps* made from potatoes and flavoured with caraway. This is often given as an antidote to someone who has eaten *hárkarl*.

1 large rack of lamb
1 tbsp dijon mustard
salt and freshly
   ground white pepper

sauce
bones from rack of lamb
2 – 3 tbsp vegetable oil
1 carrot, cut into small pieces
1 leek, cut into small pieces
1 celery stalk, cut into
   small pieces
10 black peppercorns
1 tsp sage
250 ml cream
salt to taste
2 tbsp *Dijon* mustard

mustard spiced lamb with creamed potatoes

1 Remove lamb from the bone. Make shallow cuts into the fat, then keep cool while the sauce is made. **2** Chop bones into small pieces. Heat oil in a heavy skillet and brown bones in oil on all sides. **3** Add vegetables and brown with bones. Pour in enough water to cover the bones (not more than 1 litre). **4** Add the spices to skillet and boil. Simmer at a low heat for at least 1 hour. Strain and skim off most of the fat. Reduce on low heat till 1/3 is left. **5** Add the cream and then the mustard. Bring to boil and then whisk well. **6** Heat the oven till 160 degrees Celsius. Cut the meat into 4 – 6 even pieces, season with salt and pepper. **7** Heat a heavy skillet and place meat on it with the fat layer down. Brown on all sides. **8** Smear meat with mustard and then place the meat in the oven for about 10 – 15 minutes. **9** Place meat on a hot serving plate and pour sauce over it. **10** Serves between 4 – 6.

Recipe courtesy of Chef Hilmar B Jonsson.

spaghetti puttanesca

1 In a frying pan, sauté the garlic with olive oil and cook until it turns golden. **2** Remove the garlic and add the tomatoes, stirring well. Add the capers, anchovies and pitted olives. Simmer until the sauce thickens. Add the parsley and set the sauce aside. **3** In a large pot, boil 4 litres of salted water. Cook the pasta till it is cooked but firm to the bite (*al dente*). **4** Drain and toss with the sauce. **5** Add the minced chili if desired.

italy

The Italian passion for food begins early in life with children watching fascinated as their mothers prepare meal after meal. Italians are brought up to be serious about what they eat. Food is a constant topic of discussion and regarded with the utmost respect. This is most obvious during lunch, traditionally the most important meal of the day; when everything comes to a stand still for two or three hours as families comes together to have their midday meal.

The significance of food in an Italian's life is one unifying element tying together the regional distinctions in the country. *Risotti*, in its many forms, and *polenta* made from cornmeal, grace many a table in the northern reaches of Lombardia. This cattle-growing region is also famous for beef and veal, and dishes such as *osso bucco* (braised veal shanks). Piedmonte is a meat eater's delight, known for its beef, lamb, hare, deer and game. *Grissini* (crunchy Italian breadsticks) were invented here, and prized white truffles are hunted like jewels in the Alba hills. Soups of bean and vegetable are Tuscan specialties, as is the Pecorino cheese made of sheep milk, wonderful eaten at the end of a meal.

The world has Campagnia to thank for the gift of *pizza*, originating as sailor's food in the 18th century. The quality of wheat in Sicily, on the other hand, has made pasta there legendary. In its many shapes and sizes, it is eaten Sicilian-style with plentiful sauce, vegetables, *ricotta* cheese and even breadcrumbs. Seafood is naturally popular on the island – the likes of anchovies, tuna and blue fin often showing up in *antipasti*, pasta and main courses.

A typical Italian meal begins with an *antipasto* as a starter. It may be as simple as a few delicate slices of *salami* or as elaborate and rich as *vitello tonnato* (veal in tuna fish sauce). This is followed by *il primo* (first course), which is usually pasta or a soup, and should balance and complement the preceding dish. The *secondo* or main course is usually a portion of meat or fish accompanied by either a salad or lightly cooked greens. A meal typically ends with a variety of cheeses followed by pastries or decadent dessert concoctions like *tiramisu* (biscuit fingers with brandy and *mascarpone* cheese). An Italian wine such as the robust *Barolo*, the delicate *Barbaresco*, or even the ever-popular *Chianti* invariably lifts the mood to a higher state.

500 g spaghetti
6 anchovy fillets
½ cup olive oil
4 cloves garlic
80 g black olives,
    pitted and chopped
1 tbsp capers
500 g tinned tomatoes,
    peeled
1 bunch parsley
1 red chili,
    minced finely (optional)
salt to taste
4 litres water

Abissini

Cannelloncini

Fusilli

Penne

OODLES OF NOODLES

Whether the pasta originated from Marco Polo's jaunt to the Far East will always be a topic of contention among foodies around the world. But one thing is for sure, the veritable noodle, and its derivatives, is one of the most characterising elements of Italian cuisine.

But pasta is more than the omnipresent spaghetti with which we are all too familiar. The pasta family abounds with varieties far exceeding our expectations. So, the next time you're faced with ordering a pasta dish, you might want to try one of these departures from the 'straight and narrow': *cannelloncini*, *penne*, *fusilli*, *farfallette*, *abissini*, *cappelletti* and *permanente*.

cyprus.malta.monaco

Cyprus is a sunshine island of exotic fragrances and Eastern Mediterranean flavours. Both the Turkish-influenced North and the Greek-influenced South combine to give Cypriot food its unique and traditional character.

The best way to try Cypriot food is to sample their *meze* (short for *mezedhes*, or 'little delicacies'). With up to 30 dishes are served at one sitting, this could be a meal in its own. Black and green olives; dips with fresh village bread and a bowl of *salata horiatiki* (village salad); *octapodi krasato* (octopus in red wine); grilled *halloumi* cheese and *lountza* (smoked pork); *keftedes* (meatballs); *loukanika* (smoked sausages); and *ofto kleftico* (meat baked in a sealed oven) are just some examples of this creative and exotic fare.

A deeper venture into Cypriot cuisine must include *pourgouri* (cracked wheat steamed with fried onions and chicken stock served with plain yoghurt), *koupepia* (rolled vine leaves stuffed with meat and rice), *stifado* (beef or rabbit stew cooked with onions, vinegar and wine) and *souvla* (lamb flavoured with fresh herbs and spit-roasted). Desserts include *galatopoureko*, a *filo* pastry with a cream filling and *mahalepi*, a creamy pudding, which floats on rosewater syrup. *Commandaria* is a sweet dessert wine that often complements a meal.

Food in Malta, on the other hand, is influenced mainly by the Sicilians and later, the British. Unpretentious, basic and nourishing, this is homely food at its best, produced from indigenous ingredients. *Pastizzi* (cheese-filled flakey pastry), *timpana* (a flakey pastry made with meat, macaroni, cheese and egg), along with their well-known *aljotta* (a thin and clear fish broth) and *minestra* (a chunky vegetable soup to which up to 10 varieties of vegetables and pasta are added) is typical fare. In addition, the Maltese love *fenek* (rabbit), either fried, in a casserole or baked in a pie. Bread is excellent, and a cottage loaf with a firm crisp crust and a soft white centre, is usually eaten by the Maltese *hobz biz-zejt* (dipped in oil). *Mqaret*, is a popular dessert of small diamond-shaped pastries filled with a soft date mix flavoured with aniseed, deep-fried and eaten hot.

The cosmopolitan nature of food in Monaco is inversely proportionate to the size of this Mediterranean principality. Haute cuisine of a French/!talian heritage is a main feature, but native Monegasque cuisine still has a strong foothold in this epicurean heaven. *Barbajuan* (puff pastry with vegetables and herbs), *fougasse* (sweet bread with fruits, nuts and anise), and *swiss chard pie* layered with cheese, eggs, onions and rice, and *socca* (chick pea pancakes sold by street vendors) are examples of how French Provençal and southern Italian influences have carved a unique identity of their own.

These sun-baked jewels of the Mediterranean have become havens of culinary perfection. Their European heritage has parlayed the bountiful produce of a rich land into one of the gastronomic highlights of the region.

barbajuans

pastry: 1 Combine flour and salt in a food processor. Add oil, 2 tbsp egg (reserve remaining egg for filling) and 3 tbsp water. **2** Process until a smooth dough forms, adding more water by teaspoonfuls if the dough is too dry. Turn dough out onto a lightly floured surface and knead until smooth, about 1 minute. **3** Wrap the dough in plastic and let stand 30 minutes. **filling: 4** Heat 1½ tsp olive oil in a heavy medium skillet over medium heat. Add onions and leek, and sauté until tender and golden, about 4 minutes. **5** Add chard, spinach and oregano, and sauté until very tender, about 10 minutes. **6** Transfer to a small bowl. Mix in cheeses. Season with salt and pepper. **7** Mix in 1 tbsp egg reserved from the pastry. Set filling aside to cool. **8** Line a large baking sheet with foil. Roll out the dough on a floured surface to about 3-mm in thickness. Using a floured 5 – 6-cm round cutter, cut out rounds. **9** Gather dough and re-roll, cutting out more rounds to make a total of 24. **10** Place 1 tsp of the filling in the centre of each dough-round. Brush edges of rounds with egg white. Fold dough over, forming half-circle and press edges to seal. **11** Place pastries on a prepared baking sheet. (This can be made 1 week ahead. Cover and freeze. Thaw before continuing, and pat dry if dough is wet). **12** Pour vegetable oil into a heavy large Dutch oven to a depth of 4-cm. Heat oil to 170 degrees Celsius. **13** Working in batches, fry pastries until brown and crisp, about 5 minutes. **14** Using a slotted spoon, transfer pastries to paper towels and drain. Arrange pastries on platter. **15** Serve warm or at room temperature.

pastry

1½ cups all-purpose flour
½ tsp salt
¼ cup olive oil
1 egg, beaten to blend
3 tbsp (or more) water

filling

1½ tsp olive oil
2 tbsp onion, finely chopped
2 tbsp leek, finely chopped
  (white part only)
2 Swiss chard leaves, stems
  & ribs removed, chopped
¾ cup fresh spinach, chopped
½ tsp dried oregano
2½ tbsp *ricotta* cheese
1 tbsp *Parmesan* cheese,
  freshly grated
1 egg white, beaten to blend
vegetable oil for deep frying
salt and pepper

afelia

1 Marinate the meat in the wine and spices for at least 4 hours, or preferably overnight. **2** Drain the meat and dry on kitchen paper. Save the marinade. **3** Heat the oil in a heavy casserole and brown the meat a few at a time, until all are crisp and brown. Add more oil if necessary. **4** When all the meat is fried, remove excess oil from the pan and return all the meat to it. **5** Pour the saved marinade over the meat and add enough cold water to just cover. **6** Cover the casserole with a lid and cook gently, either in a 170 degrees Celsius oven or on top of the range over medium heat for about 30 minutes, or till the meat is tender. Almost all the liquid would have evaporated leaving a thick sauce. **7** If necessary, cook the *afelia* an additional 10 minutes to reduce excess liquid.

1 kg lean pork, de-boned
  and diced
¾ cup red wine
1 – 2 tbsp coriander seeds,
  crushed coarsely
salt and black pepper
1 stick cinnamon
6 tbsp sunflower or
  vegetable oil

netherlands

Windmills and clogs might be Netherlands' unofficial cultural symbols, but the food of the land is just as distinctive. From a history steeped in farming comes a palate rich in dairy products, grains and meat. Arguably, the country's most reputed export is cheese. *Edam*, *Gouda* and *Leiden* – cheeses named after the towns from which they come – have become household varieties around the world.

Dutch main courses run the gamut of meat, fish and fresh vegetables found in the country. For the most part though, Dutch dishes – like *boerenkool* (kale with smoked sausages) and *hutspot* (mashed carrots, onions and potatoes) – still remain practically unknown outside of the Netherlands. Pancakes are the exception. Indeed, the Dutch pancake house is an institution, serving gut-stuffing renditions topped with meats, fruits, cheese and just about anything one's imagination can conjure.

Those with a sweet tooth will find the Netherlands a haven. The Dutch like their sweets and find a way to consume it regardless of time or place. Throughout the land, the popular cafés serve strong black coffee, a Dutch favourite that is the perfect foil for the likes of *boterkoek* (a strong, buttery cake), *suikerbrood* (sweet bread baked with sugar and spices), and *poffertjes* (mini-pancakes served with melted butter and powdered sugar). The southern province of Limburgh (*limburgse vlaai*) is particularly well known for their flans filled with fruit and creamed rice, and a crust made with sweet yeast dough.

At any time of day, beer remains the beverage of choice. *Bols* and *Heineken* are recognizable exports, but smaller breweries around the country are becoming popular drinking spots. *Jenever*, a Dutch gin made from juniper berries, is yet another, albeit more ethnic, pick-me-up.

Through the years, the Netherlands has opened its doors to an influx of immigrants. Notably, Indonesian foods are pervasive, and the likes of *rijstafel*, or 'rice table' (where diners sample from an exhaustive buffet of Indonesian-style dishes) have become common fare in the country.

hutspot

This traditional recipe originated from the town of Leiden. According to legend, in 1574, the siege of Leiden was lifted, and a young boy, exploring an abandoned military camp, found a pan of *hutspot*. Today, the dish is eaten in Leiden on the 3rd of October to commemorate the lifting of the siege.

1 Bring water to a boil with the salt, add beef and cook for about 1 hour. **2** Add potatoes, carrots and onions to the meat and boil, about 30 minutes or until vegetables are cooked. **3** Remove the meat from the pan and keep warm. Drain excess water from the pan into a bowl and set aside. **4** Mash potatoes and vegetables together. **5** Boil the milk with the butter and add to the potato mixture. If it is too dry, add a little of the water that was set aside earlier. **6** Cut the beef into small pieces and mix it with the vegetable mixture. **7** Serves about 3 – 4.

600 g chuck steak, (brisket or other cuts suitable for stewing may be used)
3 decilitres water
1 tbsp salt
1½ kg potatoes, peeled and quartered
1½ kg carrots, peeled and finely chopped
400 g onions, peeled and finely chopped
100 g butter or margarine
1 decilitre milk

farikal (lamb in cabbage)

In the early days, fresh mutton was only available to the very rich. Only cheaper, fattier cuts of meat were available to commoners. These they used to cook with cabbage and peppercorns into what is now considered a national dish. Of course, leaner meats may be used in today's recipes.

1 Cut the cabbage into segments. **2** Place the lamb and cabbage in layers in the saucepan, starting with the lamb. Sprinkle flour, salt and peppercorns between the layers. **3** Pour boiling water over the layers. Bring to a boil and let the lamb and cabbage simmer over low heat until the meat is tender, about 1 – 2 hours. **4** Serve *farikal* hot with plain boiled potatoes. **5** This dish is often served with beer and *Aquavit*.

1 ½ kg lamb, from neck, shank
  or breast, with bones,
  cut into serving sizes
1 ½ kg cabbage
2 tsp salt
4 tsp peppercorns
1 – 2 tbsp flour
3 decilitres water

norway

For the longest time, conventional wisdom considered Norwegian cuisine as exciting as the country's summer is long. However, food is taken seriously here and, interestingly enough, its hardy weather is the reason for some of its bounties.

The great stretch of *fjords* abutting the Norwegian and Arctic seas distinctly defines the coastline of Norway. So too does the wealth of seafood that is harvested from its icy waters. For over a thousand years, cod fished from these waters have been sold to countries in Europe in exchange for other food products. Today, a dried version called clipfish is sold as far away as in South America and the Caribbean, where it is known as *bacalao* and used in a hundred different ways.

In the cool Nordic climate, fruits and berries ripen slowly. But these give them a unique flavour. Norwegian apples, cherries and strawberries are now much sought after in the markets worldwide. Of the long list of cured, smoked, dried, salted and pickled meat and fish products, *fenalar*, a sausage of cured leg of mutton, stands out as a national specialty. The weather makes it difficult to cultivate grapes for wine, but they make up for it with beer and *Aquavit*, a liquor distilled from potatoes and often flavoured with caraway.

Globalisation has brought many different cuisines to Norway, but lately, people there are rediscovering the recipes of a generation past. Traditional dishes like *rakfish* (fermented fish), *gammelost* (sour milk cheese) and *pinnekjott* (salted lamb ribs) are rekindling a culinary history of which the Norwegians can be proud.

portugal

A tour of Portugal's culinary past may be compared to tasting the country's history – from the time of the Roman Empire, through the era of Moorish influence, to the Age of Discoveries. Portugal's long coastline and varied terrain and climate result in a vast variety of cooking styles and regional specialties.

Portuguese food is evolved from an imaginative use of local raw ingredients, coupled with a touch of exoticism. It incorporates influences from the East (pepper, clove, nutmeg and cinnamon), the New World (corn, peppers, chilies, potatoes, avocados and tomatoes), the Moors, and North Africa (many of Madeira's dishes are based on North Africa's ubiquitous *couscous*).

The use of onions, garlic, olive oil, seafood (cod in particular), and pork are often giveaways to a typical Portuguese meal. Signature dishes like *bacalhau à brás* (dried salted cod fried in olive oil with garlic and vegetables) and *bohinhos de bacalhau* (cod balls mixed with potato and fried); *carne de porco à alentejana* (pork marinated in wine and herbs, then cooked with baby clams); *tripas à modo do Porto* (tripe with haricot beans and belly pork) and *caldreirada* (a Portuguese *bouillabaisse* comprising nine varieties of fish and shellfish) are worn like national badges. The Portuguese are particularly known for *sopa* (soup) – light *canja de galinha* (chicken and rice soup), and the hearty *sopa de grão* (chickpea soup) being two worthy of mention. Sausages *choriço* and *alheiras* are also often found on the regular menu.

The Portuguese sweet tooth might have been sharpened from the time of the Moors. All-time favourites include *pudim de flan* (caramel custard), *arroz doce* (cinnamon-flavoured rice pudding) and *pudim molotov* (poached meringue with caramel or peach topping). A delectable alternative is *queijo du serra* (a soft, yet firm and strong-tasting cheese produced from ewe's milk). There are delightful wines to accompany these wonderful dishes, from the sweetish, lightly sparkling rosé wines like *Mateus Rosé*, to red and white *vinhos verdes* and *dão* wines. *Uma bica* (an *espresso*-like coffee) and *cha com leite* or *cha uma rodela de limao* (tea with milk or lemon respectively) are satisfying ways to end a typical meal that is not only built on the fine balance of numerous flavours and ingredients, but on a rich, historical heritage as well.

250 g dried salt cod (*bacalhau*)
3 medium yellow onions,
   sliced thin
2 large garlic cloves, minced
¼ cup olive oil
2 cups peanut or vegetable oil
2 medium potatoes
10 large eggs, beaten until frothy
2 tbsp parsley
12 large oil-cured black olives
pepper to taste

bacalhau a bras

1 Soak the salt cod in cold water and leave in the refrigerator for 24 hours, changing the water frequently. **2** Drain the cod, rinse thoroughly with cool water, and drain well again. Remove all the bones and skin of the salt cod, and with your fingers, shred the cod into fine shreds. Set aside. **3** Sauté the onions and garlic in the olive oil over moderate heat. Turn the heat down to low, cover and allow all the mixture to steam for about 10 minutes. **4** Add the cod, mix well, cover and cook over low heat for 25 minutes, stirring occasionally. **5** Meanwhile, cut potatoes into thin strips and fry for about a minute. Remove the potatoes and spread them over a paper towel to dry. **6** When the cod is ready, add the half-fried potato strips and cook, stirring occasionally, for about 2 minutes. **7** Add the eggs, pepper and half the parsley. Cook over moderate heat, stirring the eggs occasionally, until the eggs are set but not overcooked. **8** Place the cod/egg mixture on a heated platter, sprinkle with the remaining parsley and garnish with the black olives. **9** Serve with a green salad.

300 g short grain white rice, about 2½ cups
500 g chicken, preferably thigh meat,
  cut into small pieces
250 g lean pork, cut into small pieces
½ cup olive oil
1 large tomato, skinned, seeded and chopped
2 garlic cloves, peeled and chopped
²/₃ tsp sweet *paprika*
½ cup fresh peas, shelled
½ cup green beans, sliced
12 fresh snails, prepared
6 cups boiling stock
10 threads saffron
salt and pepper to taste
12 clams in the shell, cleaned and soaked
6 mussels in the shell, cleaned and soaked
50 g squid
6 large prawns
lemons, halved

paella valenciana

1 Season chicken and pork with salt and brown in olive oil in a *paella*, or other suitable large wide flat pan. Add tomato, garlic, *paprika* and stir on medium heat for 2 – 4 minutes. **2** Add the peas, beans and snails. Put in the rice and cook briefly. Add half the boiling stock and simmer till the rice partially absorbs the liquid. **3** Crush the saffron in a little boiling water and stir into the rice. Season to taste. **4** Add half of the remaining stock to the rice and cook for a little while. **5** Put in the shellfish, squid and prawns on top of the rice and cook till rice is tender. Add additional stock when required. When cooked, the rice should be *al dente* and slightly moist. **6** Before serving, stir the seafood into the rice and present with half lemons. **7** Serves 6.

spain

Geographically sited on a peninsula border between the Mediterranean Sea and the Atlantic Ocean, Spain is at the crossroads of civilisations and the melting pot of many cultures. Food plays an important element in the Spanish way of life. Leisurely eating is a social affair that provides pleasure and relaxation. In general, different regions characterised the food in Spain: sauces predominate in the South, casseroles in the East, peppers in the North-east, fried foods in the South, and rice in the South-east. The common fundamental principle behind Spanish food is using only the freshest ingredients.

Spain is renowned for many dishes, like the now-common *tapas* (Spanish-style bite-sized appetisers to accompany an aperitif), *paella* (a one-dish meal of saffron rice with chicken and seafood) and *gazpacho* (a cold soup of garlic, olive oil and fresh vegetables). The *cocido*, a meal-in-a-pot based on chickpeas, vegetable and meat, is generally deemed Spain's national dish. Other famous dishes include *romesco de peix* (a fish casserole), *fabada* (a bean stew made with sausage), *ternasco a la aragonesa* (Aragon style roast lamb), *arroz negro* (short-grained rice blackened with squid ink) and *bonito en salmorejo* (tuna in spicy red pepper and cumin sauce).

Tapas is a microcosm of traditional Spanish cooking, representing not just their cooking, but their lifestyle. As a rule of thumb, Spaniards love gathering in bars before a 3-hour lunch, grazing on *tapas* with beer, wine or dry (*fino*) sherry. Mouth-watering *tapas* are found all over Spain, and specially noted in Basque country, Madrid and Andalucia. Typical *tapas* include seafood salads, grilled shellfish, Spanish cured ham, *chorizo* sausage and *Manchego* cheese.

Although Andorra is technically a country unto its own, its cuisine is predominantly *Catalan* (a Spanish region), and is also influenced by France and Italy. Pasta is a familiar site with local dishes like *cunillo* (rabbit in tomato sauce), *xai* (roast lamb), and *escudella* (chicken and sausage stew) reflecting the provincial aspects of its cooking.

In a nutshell, Spanish cuisine is traditional and simple; a collection of micro-cuisine that reflects one's own village and what is grown in the immediate region. Spanish cuisine is light, fresh, healthful and delicious, with basic ingredients of olive oil, bread and rice, fresh fruit and vegetables, pulses and wine. Spanish cuisine has the honour of being accepted today as 'The Mediterranean Diet'.

gravlax (gravad lax)

Arguably, this is one of Sweden's few contributions to international cuisine. The name is actually connected with 'grave' – in the 'buried' sense, that is. During the time when salt was expensive, people would dig a deep pit, put the fish in and sprinkle a little salt over it. The fish is kept in this state for a long time to acidify and ferment.

1 Keep salmon deep-frozen for at least 24 hours and then allow to thaw before preparation. **2** Once thawed, clean and fillet the salmon. Dry well, don't rinse. Leave the skin on. **3** Mix the sugar, pepper and salt together, and rub the season into the fleshy side of the fish. **4** Put a good amount of dill onto the fleshy parts of the salmon, then put the two fillets together with the thick side against the thin. Put salmon in a plastic bag, seal and place in a refrigerator. The marinade period should last for about 36 hours. In the middle of it, turn the bag over. **5** Once ready, remove the fish and scrape away the seasoning and cut the salmon into thin slices. Garnish with lemon and dill, and serve with *gravlax* sauce. **sauce: 6** Blend the mustards, sugar and vinegar together. Add the oil, whisking all the time. **7** Season to taste with dill, salt and pepper.

sweden

The absence of Swedish restaurants around the world perhaps speaks a little about the exportability of the cuisine, long known to be dull and overly stodgy. But on closer scrutiny, Sweden's food heritage is one fraught with many unknown delights. And though conventional palates may not immediately appreciate some of the country's esoteric delicacies, these traditional dishes reflect the imagination of a people living at the mercy of the Scandinavian climate.

When we speak of Swedish *husmanskost* (home cooking) we cannot get away from classic preparations like boiled, salted loin of pork with mashed turnips, mutton and cabbage stew, and Swedish pea soup cooked with pork (usually served on a Thursday – a tradition from medieval times). Apart from these simple fares, Swedish cooking has also been influenced by culinary ideas from other countries. The Swedish *smorgasbord* (a buffet spread of cold and cooked foods popular in Scandinavia), also known as *brannvinsbord*, is a rendition of a Russian practice of snacking on *hors d'oeuvres* before a meal. Swedish *schnapps* (called *braanvin*) is also borrowed from the Russian art of distilling liquor from grain.

Characteristic long winters have led the Swedes to revel during the limited seasons when land and sea are ripe for harvest. In late summer, when crayfish are bountiful, shops around the country display all manner of crayfish paraphernalia in celebration of the country's partiality to the crimson crustacean. And autumn is the season for eel parties where eel prepared in a myriad of ways – fried, grilled, smoked and stuffed, to name a few – is served. November in the southern province of Skane will see roast geese served with 'black' soup (made of geese blood) and *spettkaka*, a desert made from eggs yolks and sugar cooked on a skewer over an open fire.

1 kg salmon, preferably
   from the middle of the fish
4 tbsp sugar
4 tbsp sea salt
2 tsp white peppercorns,
   coarsely crushed
1 large bunch of dill, chopped

gravlax sauce (*gravlaxsas*)
2 – 3 tbsp *Scanian* mustard
1 tsp *Dijon* mustard
1 – 2 tbsp sugar
$^2/_5$ cup oil
1 – 2 tbsp vinegar
3 tbsp dill, finely chopped
salt and pepper to taste

garnish
lemon wedges
dill

north
america

1

2

1 medium-size turkey,
   whole and thawed

dry dressing
2 cups white bread crumbs
2 cups corn bread crumbs
1 onion, chopped
$^2/_3$ cup celery, chopped
2 eggs, beaten
$^1/_3$ cup butter, melted
seasoning to taste
stock to moisten

roast turkey and stuffing

Thanksgiving is one of America's favourite holidays. It is usually celebrated with family get-togethers and an abundance of good food. Thanksgiving is also not complete without roast turkey and stuffing. Each family has its own recipe, often passed down from generation to generation.

1 Combine all dressing ingredients into a bowl. Pour in melted butter and mix. Moisten the dressing with hot stock, just enough for the dressing to hold together. **2** Pre-heat oven to 175 degrees Celsius. Stuff cavity of turkey with dressing. **3** Place turkey in the oven and bake for 15 minutes per ½ kilogram.

usa

From 'sea to shining sea', the culinary landscape of the United States is defined by its numerous migrant cultures. Over the last two centuries of American history, people from every continent have made this their home, bringing along not only their beliefs but their food as well. Today, what may be termed 'American food' is a topic of perennial discussion. The conclusions are indeterminable at best, and for the most part, inconsequential. For what is offered in this 'land of plenty' is a vast spectrum of delicacies reflecting the best of America's vibrant population.

Food in almost every part of the world is easily found in any city in the continental USA. But that does not mean that regional characteristics do not exist within the American context. In the Northeast, European influence is a throwback from when the first pilgrims from Europe landed. Rich farmlands in the Midwest have meant a diet defined by fresh produce and livestock, and grazing prairies in the central and southwestern parts of the continent have propagated an affinity towards barbecued meats.

Hispanic influence in regional cuisines is easily discernible in Florida where there lives a large Cuban community. In Texas, Arizona and most of the Southwest, cooking styles and ingredients from neighbouring Mexico have created a hybrid genre, now popularly known as Tex-Mex. While in the deep South, the Cajun and Creole cuisines of New Orleans are internationally renown as unique blends of French and Afro-American influences. In the northwest states of Washington and Oregon, Native American methods of preparing fish – like the *potlatch* (skewered fish roasted over an open fire) – were the precursors of a regional cuisine rich in the 'fruits of the sea'.

Culinary influences in America do not necessarily have to come from cultural sources. In California, a penchant for health and the avant garde has led to the birth of 'California Cuisine' – a term often associated with creative use of fresh produce prepared with the minimal use of cholesterol-laden ingredients. This, and the fertile wine growing valleys of Napa have raised the culinary significance of this state to global prominence.

At the end of the day, America is a land where people from different origins live under a common rule. In their very own way, each and every one of them hold on to their roots, in no small part, by virtue of the bounties they bring to the varied topography of American cuisine.

grilled chicken with beer and maple syrup

1 In a large pan, reduce the beer by half; cool. **2** In a large bowl, stir together the beer, maple syrup, tropical fruit juice, soya sauce, mustard, green onion, garlic and savory. **3** Add the chicken pieces, turn to coat on all sides and marinate in the refrigerator for at least 4 hours. **4** Drain the chicken pieces well, season and grill on the barbecue for 20 – 25 minutes over medium-hot coals; brush the chicken pieces with the remaining marinade during the grilling. **5** Serve with vegetable kebabs and a green salad.

canada

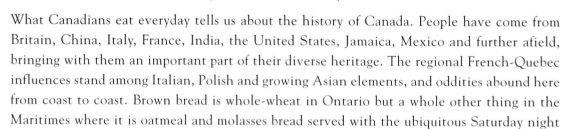

The jury still appears to be out when it comes to deciding what Canadian food truly is. Yet, food reflects the country's history as an immigrant nation – a layered casserole of the multiculturalism that Canadians get a taste of each day.

What Canadians eat everyday tells us about the history of Canada. People have come from Britain, China, Italy, France, India, the United States, Jamaica, Mexico and further afield, bringing with them an important part of their diverse heritage. The regional French-Quebec influences stand among Italian, Polish and growing Asian elements, and oddities abound here from coast to coast. Brown bread is whole-wheat in Ontario but a whole other thing in the Maritimes where it is oatmeal and molasses bread served with the ubiquitous Saturday night treat of baked beans and molasses.

In Ontario they like baked beans in tomato sauce. Salt pork is a staple in Maritime kitchens (at least it can be found at the grocery store) but not so in Ontario. From the classic list of cherries jubilee, Swedish pancakes, beef *stroganoff*, Peking duck, veal *scallopini* and chicken *Morney*, to original Canadian cuisine of *naniamo* bars and tomato soup cake – many connoisseurs have concluded that Canadian food is as all encompassing as it is diverse. Call it fusion or colonial cuisine; what remains is a culinary imagination that grows richer with time.

Most recognisable of Canadian dining is probably the proud symbol of the Canadian flag – the maple leaf. In the Spring, when the days turn warmer, the sun shines longer and the nights are cool, the sap rises in the maple trees and the annual tapping of the trees for maple syrup begins. All over the country maple syrup festivals and pancake breakfasts are held. School children are taken on tours of the sugar bush. A highlight of their visit is hot maple syrup poured over fresh clean snow. What a treat!

375 g beer
⅓ cup maple syrup
½ cup tropical fruit juice
1 tbsp soya sauce
1 tbsp *Dijon* mustard
1 green onion, thinly sliced
½ tsp garlic, chopped
½ tsp savory
1 1½ kg chicken,
   cut into pieces
salt and pepper to taste

central
america

1 BELIZE 2 COSTA RICA

3 EL SALVADOR 4 GUATEMALA

5 HONDURAS 6 MEXICO

7 NICARAGUA 8 PANAMA

6

1

4 5

3 7

2

8

central america

Among the countries on the Central American belt, the cuisines of Costa Rica and Guatemala stand out as two of the most distinctive. Food of Costa Rica – known for its natural beauty and friendly people – is generally based on beef, chicken and fish, accompanied by rice, corn, beans and fresh fruit. Two key common ingredients include *condimentos mixtos* (mixed seasoning) and sauces containing corn flour, salt, garlic, black pepper, onion, coriander, *paprika* and red chili. Corn and rice are staples and are found in almost every meal. The national Costa Rican dish is *gallo pinto* (black beans and rice seasoned with onions, sweet pepper and fresh coriander) and is usually eaten for breakfast, followed by fried eggs, cheese, sour cream and hot *tortillas* (unleavened cornmeal pancake). Another signature dish is *picadillos*, a delectable stew made of diced potatoes mixed with finely chopped meat, tomatoes, onions, fresh coriander and bell peppers. As a matter of practice, all meals end with coffee. And the Costa Rican coffee bean is ranked among the finest in the world.

One will find the food in Guatemala to be similar to that of Mexico. Though there is a plentiful supply of *tortillas* and *tacos*, the best of the country's food may be found in their delightfully savoury *antojitos* ('little whims'). Examples of these include the *burrito* (a *tortilla* wrapped around any combination of beans, cheese, meat, chicken or seafood, and seasoned with *salsa* or chili), the *tamale* (steamed corn dough stuffed with meat, beans chilies and wrapped in corn husks) and *tostada* (flat crisp *tortilla* topped with meat or cheese, tomatoes, beans and lettuce).

In Belize, the staples of rice and beans are given a local tropical flavour with the addition of coconut milk and fried plantains. Accompanied by chicken, beef, fish or vegetables, it makes for a hearty meal. In addition, exotic favourites like armadillo, venison and *paca* (a small brown-spotted guinea pig-like creature) tend to show up at the dining table as an occasional treat. In El Salvador, the standard daily fare is *casamiento* (rice and beans) and *pupusas* (cornmeal stuffed with farmer's cheese, refried beans or *chicharron* (fried pork fat)). Their meals are usually accompanied by *licuados* (fruit drinks), coffee and *gaseosas* (soft drinks). A typical Nicaraguan dish comprises eggs or meat, beans and rice, salad (cabbage and tomatoes), *tortillas* and seasonal fruit. For the Panamanians, rice is their daily staple and is usually eaten with meat, a salad or sometimes with barbecued bananas or plantains roasted with cinnamon and honey. A signature dish is *sancocho*, a traditional soup made with chicken and *ñame* (a root vegetable).

The food of Central America is predominantly built around rice and beans, and to a large extent, corn and its many variants. Main dishes are often accented with peppers, chilies and fresh herbs like coriander. The cuisines of each of the countries are like children from the same parents: possessing of great similarities, but each individual in its own way.

carimanolas

The main feature of this Panamanian entrée is the *yucca* – root vegetable often featured in Central American cuisine.

1 To make stuffing: season the ground meat with salt, onion, garlic, sugar and parsley. Fry in hot oil and when brown, add the tomato paste. Allow to cook over low heat till tender. Set aside. **2** Boil *yucca* with salt, not allowing it to get too soft. Grind it into a pulp while still hot and knead with salt and the lard. Add flour if necessary. **3** Form balls, flatten and fill each with the stuffing. Shape into ovals and seal well. **4** Deep fry in hot oil till golden brown.

1½ kg *yucca*
200 g ground meat
    or pork
salt to taste, diluted in
    a little water
½ onion
1 garlic clove
2 tsp tomato paste
3 tbsp lard
⅛ tsp sugar
parsley
sifted flour if dough is
    too sticky
oil for deep frying

churrasco

1 Season beef fillets with pepper, garlic salt and onion salt. Grill over charcoal till desired doneness. **2** Prepare a sauce by combining the tomatoes, onions, herbs, salt, vinegar and orange juice. **3** Serve the beef fillets and sauce separately.

1 kg beef fillet, sliced thickly
1 tbsp garlic salt
1 tbsp onion salt
½ tbsp pepper

sauce
6 tomatoes, finely chopped
3 onions, finely chopped
5 tbsp herbs, chopped
    (e.g. basil, rosemary,
    thyme, parsley)
1½ tsp salt
juice from 1 sour orange
1 tsp vinegar

jocon

1 Cook chickens with salt, onions, tomatoes and garlic. **2** Liquefy the coriander, chili peppers, small green tomatoes and the welsh onions with a little bit of chicken broth. **3** Fry this mixture with a little oil over low heat. Thicken with the corn powder until a desired consistency is obtained, neither too watery nor too thick. **4** Split the chicken into pieces and put in the cooked mixture for 10 minutes. **5** Serve hot with white rice.

2 large chickens
2 onions, chopped
1 bunch coriander
4 green chili peppers
1 cup juice of small
    green tomatoes
6 stalks welsh onions
250 g corn powder
3 garlic cloves
2 tomatoes
salt to taste

mexico

Mexican food must rank as one of the world's most misrepresented cuisines. In truth, the cuisine of Mexico is a rich tapestry of fresh ingredients and varied cooking methods – a far cry from the *burritos* and *enchiladas* frequently found in Tex-Mex restaurants around the world.

Mexico is a large country with over 90 million people and a geography that encompasses coastal areas, deserts, rainforests and fertile valleys. As a result, its food reflects the great diversity of this bountiful land and a rich history of gastronomic significance. As with most countries with a colonial past, Mexican cuisine is influenced greatly by its immigrant rulers – in this case, the Spanish. Prior to the arrival of the Spaniards, the native Indians were ignorant of frying their food, only using the methods of steaming, grilling, boiling and an ingenious method known as *pib* (steam cooking meat in earthen ovens dug in the soil). Spanish conquest in the 16th century also brought foodstuffs such as pork, beef, chicken, olives, onions, and dairy products like cheese, eggs, butter and cream. Today, these 'imports' have become commonplace at the Mexican dining table.

Mexico, itself, has introduced many ingredients to the world: chocolate, tomato, avocados, peanuts, *jicama* and vanilla, to name a few. But it is corn that features most prominently in all foods Mexican. In ancient times, corn formed the core of religious rituals and daily life. Today, hardly a day goes by that a Mexican does not consume it in one of its many forms: in a *tortilla*, stew, dessert, or even a drink.

If we are what we eat, then the zest for life found in the Mexican people may just originate from their insatiable consumption of chili. *Habanero, joto, macho, hungaro* — they come in many shapes and sizes, and degrees of hotness. This fiery band is used in as many ways as one's creativity can muster: pickled, added to *salsa*, in sauces, or straight up no chaser. The topography of Mexico drapes the land like a colourful blanket, providing a wealth of indigenous produce and inspiration for a myriad of regional specialties. Seafood from the Gulf Shore, ancient *criollo* (native Indian) dishes from the Isthmus area, hearty meat dishes from the North, and wines from Baja California, to name a few, all provide a culinary patchwork of the country's well-endowed heritage.

A people's attitude towards their food is often a mirror to their beliefs. The time and labour-intensive ways in which the Mexican prepare their favourite dishes – most of which require laborious preparation and can include up to 30 different spices – and the common practice of close ones sitting down together for a meal, is a window to the importance granted the family and community.

mole poblano

If there is one typical Mexican dish, it must be *mole*. The name originates from the Nahuatl word *mulli*, which means 'sauce'. One legend speaks of a sister, Sor Andrea de la Asuncion, in a convent who invented it to be served to a visiting viceroy, Count Paredes y Marques de la Laguna, in the eighteenth century. The dish is served on special occasions such as birthdays, weddings and baptisms.

sauce: 1 Heat a little lard in a large, deep saucepan. Fry halved onion till transparent and slightly brown, add garlic cloves and brown. Remove and reserve the garlic. **2** Add more lard, fry chopped onion, garlic head, tomatoes and tomatillos. Remove and set aside. **3** Add more lard, fry sesame seeds, almonds, peanuts, raisins, prunes, plantains, coriander seed, anise and cinnamon. Remove. **4** Dry all fried ingredients with paper towels and put them, together with the *croissant*, *tortillas* and broth in a blender or food processor. Blend thoroughly. **5** Heat the remaining lard and brown onion slices. Add the blended ingredients and salt, and simmer over low heat for about 1 hour, stirring occasionally. **chilies: 1** Blend chilies *mulattos*, *anchos*, *pasillas*, and *chipotle* in a blender with onion, garlic and a little reserved soaking water. **2** Strain the mixture and stir gradually into the simmering spice mixture. Wait about 10 minutes between each addition of the chilies. **3** Add chocolate and sugar, and salt to taste. **4** Simmer *mole* for 2 to 3 hours. Add broth until the *mole* is slightly thick. The *mole* is ready when it becomes very thick and there is a thick layer of fat on the top. Taste and add salt if required. **chicken: 1** Heat water in a large stockpot. Add chicken, onions, garlic, carrots, celery, bay leaves and salt. Cook over low heat for about 30 minutes. **2** Let the chicken cool in the broth, then remove the chicken and add the pieces to *mole* sauce and cook for 30 minutes. **3** Garnish chicken *mole* with toasted sesame seeds sprinkled over the top. **4** The dish is often served with red rice, *frijoles de olla*, and freshly made *tortillas*.

HOT STUFF

Mexicans like it hot. Breakfast, lunch, or dinner, a meal is not complete without the fiery presence of their beloved chili. There are actually over 200 species identified around the world, and, undoubtedly, many more grow in remote regions of Mexico and South America. The following is a brief primer on some varieties that have found their ways into the delicacies of the country.

Habanero – The name means 'from Havana'. When ripe, its colour varies from dark green to orange, orange-red or red. Arguably the hottest chili grown in the world. Mixes well with foods containing fruits or tomatoes.

Jalapeno – Named after Jalapa, a town in the Mexican state of Veracruz. Perhaps the most widely eaten chili in the USA. This chili may be green or red and is used in anything from *salsas* and stews to being toppings for snacks.

Manzana – Yellow-orange in colour and is also known as *chile rocoto*, *chile peron* or *chile caballo*. Soft, meaty and has a fruity flavour. Often used in sauces or stuffed (as in *chile rellenos*).

Poblano – The green version is the most popular fresh chili in Mexico. It is dark green with a purplish black tinge. Growing up to 13 cm long, its medium hot flavour is suitable for sauces and *moles*. When dried, it is called *ancho*.

sauce

2 – 3 cups lard

2½ white onions, halved

1 white onion, roasted & chopped

8 cloves garlic, whole

1 head garlic, roasted & peeled

3 tomatoes, roasted

10 *tomatillos*, roasted

¾ cup sesame seeds

¾ cup raw almonds

¾ cup raw peanuts

¾ cup raisins

1 cup prunes, pitted

1½ ripe plantains, peeled
   and sliced 5-mm thick

1 tsp coriander seed

1 tsp anise

2 sticks cinnamon

1 *croissant*, in pieces

2 charred *tortillas*, in pieces

1½ quarts hot chicken broth

2 slices white onion

salt to taste

chilies

30 chilies *mulattos* seeded
   and de-veined

16 chilies *anchos*

6 long chilies *pasillas*

1 chili *chipotle*, roasted
   or lightly fried & soaked

1½ white onions, halved

6 cloves garlic

salt to taste

230 g Mexican chocolate
   tablets (containing cinnamon),
   in pieces

¼ cup sugar

2 – 2¼ quarts hot chicken broth

chicken

5 quarts water

6 chicken thighs

12 chicken breasts, halved
   or 2 turkeys cut in pieces

2 large white onions, halved

1 head garlic, halved

3 carrots, peeled

½ rib celery

6 bay leaves

salt to taste

garnish

2 cups sesame seeds, toasted

caribbean

2 BAHAMAS

4 CUBA

10 SAINT KITTS AND NEVIS

1 ANTIGUA AND BARBUDA

8 HAITI   6 DOMINICAN REPUBLIC

5 DOMINICA

11 SAINT LUCIA

9 JAMAICA

12 SAINT VINCENT AND THE GRENADINES

3 BARBADOS

7 GRENADA

13 TRINIDAD AND TOBAGO

1 ANTIGUA AND BARBUDA

2 BAHAMAS 3 BARBADOS

4 CUBA 5 DOMINICA

6 DOMINICAN REPUBLIC

7 GRENADA 8 HAITI 9 JAMAICA

10 SAINT KITTS AND NEVIS

11 SAINT LUCIA

12 SAINT VINCENT AND

THE GRENADINES

13 TRINIDAD AND TOBAGO

eastern caribbean

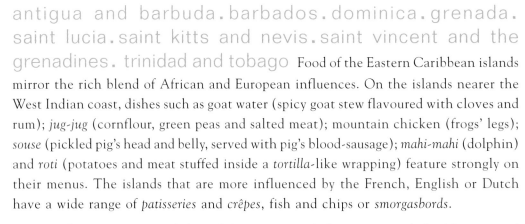

antigua and barbuda.barbados.dominica.grenada. saint lucia.saint kitts and nevis.saint vincent and the grenadines. trinidad and tobago Food of the Eastern Caribbean islands mirror the rich blend of African and European influences. On the islands nearer the West Indian coast, dishes such as goat water (spicy goat stew flavoured with cloves and rum); *jug-jug* (cornflour, green peas and salted meat); mountain chicken (frogs' legs); *souse* (pickled pig's head and belly, served with pig's blood-sausage); *mahi-mahi* (dolphin) and *roti* (potatoes and meat stuffed inside a *tortilla*-like wrapping) feature strongly on their menus. The islands that are more influenced by the French, English or Dutch have a wide range of *patisseries* and *crêpes*, fish and chips or *smorgasbords*.

In general, some signature dishes of this region include pepper pot (a highly seasoned stew of meat and peppers); *riz au djon djon* (rice with mushrooms); *soupe au fruit de pain* (breadfruit soup); flying fish prepared in a variety of ways; stuffed crab back (shell of crab stuffed with crabmeat and Creole seasonings); and a myriad of curries. Some typical beverages include rum (the national alcohol of choice), drunk neat, on ice or in cocktails; divine fresh fruit juices and Cane Spirit Rothschild (CSR) mixed with Ting, a bubbly grapefruit soda.

saltfish and antrobers
(salted cod fish and eggplant)

1 Arrange the prepared salted fish, hard-boiled eggs and eggplant on a serving platter. 2 To prepare the sauce: Heat the oil in a saucepan. Fry the garlic, onion and tomatoes for about 2 – 3 minutes; then add the tomato paste and margarine. Add salt, pepper and hot sauce to taste. 3 To serve, pour the sauce over the salted fish, eggs and eggplant and serve with lettuce, fresh tomatoes and cucumber slices.

500 g salted codfish, soaked, boiled and de-boned
2 eggs, hard-boiled and sliced
500 g eggplant, cooked and chopped

sauce
4 tomatoes
1 onion, sliced
2 tbsp tomato paste
2 tbsp vegetable oil
salt and pepper to taste
¼ tsp garlic, chopped
2 tbsp margarine
hot sauce

2 cups West Indian sweet
  potato (not yams), grated
2 cups coconut, freshly grated
2 cups pumpkin, freshly grated
1 1/2 cups flour
brown sugar to taste
2 tsp vanilla essence
1 tsp ground cinnamon
pinch of salt
100 g raisins
milk to moisten
banana leaves or aluminum foil
1/2 tsp grated nutmeg
water for boiling

antigua doucouna

1 Sift flour, salt and spices in a bowl. Add grated potato, coconut and pumpkin. Mix well. Add sugar and all other ingredients. Blend to a thick consistency, adding as much milk as necessary. **2** Spoon mixture onto squares of banana leaves or foil. Tie or wrap tightly. Cook on stovetop in a pot of rapidly boiling water until contents of wrapper are firm and cooked.

fungee

This is a starch often eaten with fried fish dishes as well as grilled sausages. The cornmeal used should neither be too coarse nor too fine. If only coarse cornmeal is available, replace 1/2 cup of it with plain flour.

3 okras, cut into
  small pieces
4 cups water
3/4 tsp salt
2 cups cornmeal
1 tsp margarine
1/4 cup cold water

1 Cook okra pieces in 4 cups of salted water till soft, approximately 10 minutes. Remove okra, and let stand. **2** Remove half of the water after it has reached boiling point, set aside. **3** Wet cornmeal with cold water (the consistency should be like wet sand). Add the cornmeal to the pot with the boiling water all at once and stir with a wooden spatula. Cook on low heat till a thick paste is formed. **4** After about 5 minutes, add the okra and continue stirring under low heat, taking care to crush the okra into the cornmeal. **5** Use a sweeping motion to turn the *fungee* to the side of the pot until the whole concoction is smooth. Add additional hot water little by little to make the paste smooth. Be careful not to make it too soft. The *fungee* is cooked when it leaves the bottom of the pot without sticking to it. **6** When this happens, add 1/2 tsp margarine to it, give it a couple more turns then remove from the heat. **7** If the *fungee* is not cooked after 15 minutes of turning, add a little hot water, cover the pot and allow it to cook for 3 – 4 minutes over low heat. Resume the turning process thereafter. **8** To serve, add a little butter or margarine in a small bowl, add a piece of hot *fungee* and roll it into a ball. **9** Turn out on a warm platter and repeat the process till all the *fungee* is used up. **10** Serve with grilled sausages or prepared cod fish.

western caribbean

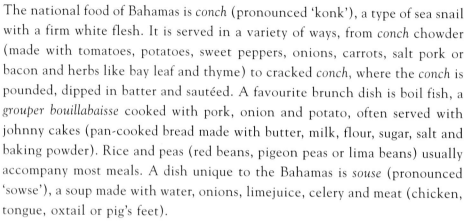

bahamas.cuba.dominican republic.haiti These nations may share the crystal clear waters, sandy beaches and tropical weather of the Caribbean, but their cuisines stand out in their own right.

The national food of Bahamas is *conch* (pronounced 'konk'), a type of sea snail with a firm white flesh. It is served in a variety of ways, from *conch* chowder (made with tomatoes, potatoes, sweet peppers, onions, carrots, salt pork or bacon and herbs like bay leaf and thyme) to cracked *conch*, where the *conch* is pounded, dipped in batter and sautéed. A favourite brunch dish is boil fish, a *grouper bouillabaisse* cooked with pork, onion and potato, often served with johnny cakes (pan-cooked bread made with butter, milk, flour, sugar, salt and baking powder). Rice and peas (red beans, pigeon peas or lima beans) usually accompany most meals. A dish unique to the Bahamas is *souse* (pronounced 'sowse'), a soup made with water, onions, limejuice, celery and meat (chicken, tongue, oxtail or pig's feet).

La bandera (the flag) is a typical Dominican Republic meal made of rice, red beans, stewed meat, salad, fried green plantains and juice. *Sancocho de siete carnes* (seven-meat soup) is another signature dish made of a hearty combination of sausage, chicken, beef, goat, salt pork, pork chops (smoked and fresh) and many vegetables. Other favourites in the Dominican Republic include *patitas de puerco guisadas en salsa de tomate* (pig's feet stewed in tomato sauce) and *pierna de chivo asada con cilantro* (roast leg of goat with coriander). *Batidas* (smoothies made of crushed fruit, ice, water and loads of sugar) and *mabí* (a refreshing drink made from the tropical liana vine) are refreshing drinks of choice across the Caribbean island.

Castro's communist rule has not eradicated Cuban cuisine from its Spanish and African influences. Signature dishes here include *Moro y Cristianos* (Moors and Christians, also known as black beans and rice), *arroz con pollo* (rice with grilled chicken) and soups made with plantains, chickpeas or beans. Their *cerveza* (Cuban beer) is especially noteworthy and will go exceptionally well with a hand-rolled *stogie*.

johnny cakes

1 Sift the dry ingredients and form a well. Rub the butter into the flour, and then add the eggs and sufficient water to make a firm dough. Knead well, and then allow to rest for 30 minutes. 2 Gently flatten to a height of 5 cm and bake in an oven on moderate heat for approximately 35 minutes.

1 kg flour
60 g baking powder
120 g sugar
1 tsp salt
4 eggs
120 g butter
nutmeg
water

peas and rice

60 g pork
30 g oil
60 g celery
60 g onion
60 g green pepper
120 g tomato paste
350 g pigeon peas
  or canned kidney
  beans
4 cups water
500 g rice
salt, pepper and
  thyme to taste

1 Cut the pork and vegetables into 1-cm cubes. Fry the pork in the oil until brown. 2 Add the vegetables and cook for 3 minutes. 3 Add the tomato paste, peas, thyme, water and seasonings to taste. Bring to a boil and add the rice. 4 Cover pan and cook for approximately 20 minutes.

shrimp in creamy coriander sauce

1 Melt butter over low heat in a skillet. When it begins to foam, add the garlic, tomatoes, coriander, sherry and shrimp, and cook, stirring, for 4 to 5 minutes. 2 To prepare the sauce: Melt butter in a saucepan over low heat. When it foams, add the flour and cook, stirring, until well blended but not brown. Increase the heat to medium, whisk in the stock and milk, until the mixture comes to a boil. 3 Add the salt, pepper, *Tabasco* and *Worcestershire*. 4 Add the sauce to the shrimp and cook over low heat for about 4 minutes. 5 Remove and serve with steamed white rice. 6 Serves 6.

3 tbsp salted butter
2 garlic cloves, finely
  chopped
2 large ripe tomatoes,
  peeled, de-seeded
1½ tsp fresh coriander
  leaves, finely chopped
¼ cup dry sherry
1 kg shrimp, shelled and
  de-veined

sauce
4 tbsp salted butter
3 tbsp all-purpose flour
1 cup fish stock or clam juice
1 cup milk
salt and freshly ground black
  pepper to taste
a dash of *Tabasco* sauce
½ tsp *Worcestershire* sauce

jamaica

Jamaican food is proud, diverse and exotic – much like the colourful Caribbean landscape from which it springs. Jamaica, the third largest island in the Caribbean, is perfectly suited to produce numerous types of fruit and vegetables, though much of these are grown by small-scale farmers who mix limes, mangoes, *ackees*, sugar cane, sweet and sour sops and anything else that will take root in their plots.

A day in Jamaica typically starts with the Jamaican national dish, *ackee* and salted fish. The mild flavor of the *ackee*, a reddish-orange fruit that can kill if it is consumed before it's fully ripe, contrasts perfectly with the robust flavour of the salted fish. Through the day, Jamaicans can be found snacking on a variety of aromatic snacks like *patties* (spicy beef, chicken or fish filled pies) and, *stamp and go* (crispy salted fish flavoured batter served with a variety of piquant sauces).

The world-famous delicacy, *jerk*, comes from marinating meats, seafood and vegetables in a spicy sauce and barbecuing it over an aromatic wood fire. Although prepared in total secrecy up to the 1950's by escaped slaves called the Maroons, jerk is now available in every village, port and town.

Jamaican legend has it that rum was discovered by an extremely thirsty slave who drank from a trash pool. Today, 4.5 million gallons of rum is produced in Jamaica each year. Not only is it drunk as an indulgence and added to numerous dishes but it's also used as a rub to treat fevers and prevent colds. A sprinkle of rum is also believed to ward off spirits and the dreaded evil eye.

The Blue Mountains, a majestic range of hills along the eastern end of Jamaica, is home to the most expensive coffee in the world: Jamaican Blue Mountain. Untouched by frost or snow, the slopes of the Blue Mountain are ideal for cultivating this subtle coffee that has become the drink of sophistication in Jamaica.

500 g saltfish, de-boned
2 dozen *ackee* pods
6 bacon slices, cut up
1 Scotch bonnet or *jalapeno* pepper, seeded and sliced
2 scallions, chopped
1 medium onion, chopped
1 medium tomato, finely chopped
½ tsp black pepper, freshly ground
1 quart water

ackee and saltfish

The *ackee* is a fruit of West African origin and this dish is considered the 'national dish' of Jamaica. It is eaten at breakfast, or as an appetiser at lunch or dinner. The fruit is available fresh or canned on the island and resembles scrambled eggs when cooked.

1 Soak the saltfish in cold water for 30 minutes, then place in a pot with 1 quart of water. Bring to boil, then drain, and break the fish into flakes. **2** Remove *ackees* from pods, discard the seeds and gently remove pink membranes with a knife. **3** Parboil the pegs of the *ackee* by covering them with salted water in a medium saucepan and bringing to boil. Remove pan from heat, drain *ackees* and set aside. **4** Fry bacon in a skillet, then reduce heat to medium-low. Add hot pepper, scallions and onion, sauté till onion is tender. **5** Stir in *ackees*, along with flaked saltfish, tomatoes and black pepper. Cook over low heat for 5 minutes. **6** Remove saltfish mixture with slotted spoon and serve with boiled or pan-fried plantains.

south
america

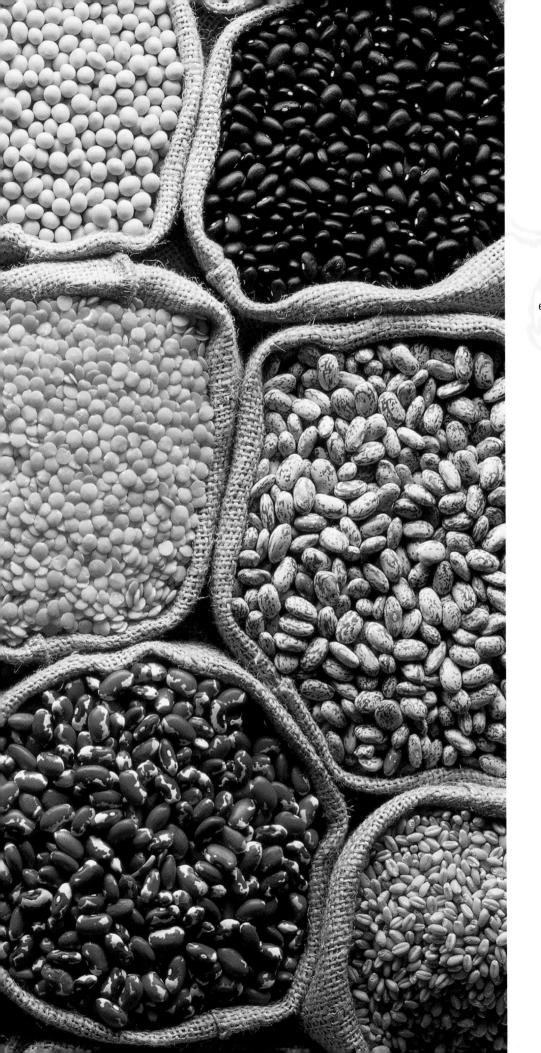

1 ARGENTINA 2 BOLIVIA

3 BRAZIL 4 CHILE

5 COLOMBIA 6 ECUADOR

7 GUYANA 8 PARAGUAY

9 PERU 10 SURINAME

11 URUGUAY 12 VENEZUELA

argentina

All across the pampas of Argentina, the image of the lone gaucho evokes a rugged romanticism of a bygone era. Strapping in his trademark hat and knee-length trousers, *boleadoras* (three stones tied with rope and used to entangle the legs of cattle) hanging by their side, these cowboys work the vast Argentine beef-growing regions around Buenos Aires, La Pampa and Cordova. An *asado* invariably ends a hard day's work for these roaming nomads – a barbecue of beef over an open fire that has since become a national icon. Argentines love their beef and at one time, devoured up to 100 kg of beef per person per year!

In Argentina, an invitation to a *mateada* is a symbol of acceptance and friendship. *Mate*, a drink similar to herbal tea, is taken through a metal spout, or *bombilla*, of a receptacle traditionally made from gourd. Friends and guests show their goodwill by drinking from a single mate. This unique practice is also found in Brazil, Paraguay and Uruguay.

Argentina is a land of natural beauty and abundance. It is currently the sixth most important food producer in the world, and is widely known for its natural methods of food cultivation. It is also the fifth largest wine producer in the world, with vineyards concentrated mostly in the region surrounding Mendoza, Salta and La Rioja.

The development of Argentina as a country has been strongly influenced by immigrants from Europe. The Italians form the majority and today their cuisine is an integral part of the Argentine culinary landscape. Interestingly, Welsh immigrants make up a significant part of the population in the South. Travelers to the region will be met with traditional British-style teahouses serving all manners of cakes and tea reminiscent of a land half a world away.

filling
1½ kg beef, topside, minced
2 kg onions, chopped
6 eggs, hard-boiled and
   chopped
1 bunch spring onions,
   chopped
270 g olives, sliced
100 g raisins, soaked in
   water (optional)
6 tbsps olive oil
2 cups water
4 cubes beef stock
cumin to taste
salt and pepper to taste

dough
2 kg plain flour
1⅓ cups olive oil
⅓ salt
1 egg mixed with about
   2 tbsps water, beaten
   and used for coating

beef empanadas

Empanadas is a typical food of the *criollos*, Argentines descendant from the first Spanish immigrants. It is also commonly found in other South American countries. The filling may consist of ham and cheese, vegetables, chicken, or tuna fish. However, the true *empanadas* is filled with beef.

Filling: **1** Heat 2 tbsps of olive oil in a pan and fry chopped onions till soft. **2** Separately, heat the remaining oil in another pan and fry the beef till it changes colour. **3** Add the fried onions to the beef, then pour in the water and beef stock cubes, and bring to a light boil. **4** Add cumin, salt and pepper to taste and cook till beef stock cubes are dissolved, about 5 – 8 minutes, and all ingredients are well incorporated. **5** Turn off the fire and spread the cooked ingredients in a flat baking tin to cool. **6** Sprinkle the chopped eggs, sliced olives, raisins and chopped spring onions into the cooked ingredients. Set aside till ready to use.

empanadas dough: **1** Mix plain flour with salt. Put the mixture in the centre of the table. Make a hole in the mixture (shaped like a volcano) then add olive oil and some water in the hole. **2** Knead the mixture for about 20 minutes and, if too dry, add a little lukewarm water. Dough must be firm, light in colour and not too watery. **3** Roll dough into a log and cut into small pieces like the size of a baby's fist. Flatten the cut dough into circular shapes with a rolling pin. **4** Place about 2 heaping tbsp of the filling onto the dough and fold into a half-circle. Fold in the edges in a crimped fashion to seal. **5** Grease a baking tin with olive oil and place the *empanadas* on it. Brush the top of the *empanadas* with the egg wash mixture. **6** Bake for approximately 30 minutes at about 150 degrees Celsius, till the *empanadas* are golden brown.

brazil

The Brazilian reputation for passion stems from the richness and exuberance present in every aspect of Brazilian culture – from its sultry music and dance, to its vibrant and unique cuisine. Shaped not only by native Indian and colonial Portuguese cooking traditions, Brazilian food has been given a truly eclectic spin through the extensive influence of her immigrants from Europe, Africa, the Middle East and Asia.

Despite this diversity, the staples of choice all over Brazil are beans, rice and manioc (cassava) meal or *farinha*. Generally served twice a day, many Brazilians would not consider a meal proper unless these are available. Although Brazil is the largest producer of beans in the world, amazingly it sometimes finds it necessary to import even more for consumption!

The black bean, the most popular bean, is indispensable in the preparation of the national dish *feijaoda* (a stew of beans, cured meats and *offal*), a recipe that varies not just from region to region, but from household to household.

The single largest influence on Brazilian cuisine is undoubtedly African in origin. Afro-Brazilian cooking is characterised by lavish use of *dende* oil (palm oil), used extensively in dishes such as *moqueca* (a fish stew wrapped in banana leaves and roasted on coals).

Also impossible to miss is the extremely hot *malagueta* pepper, widely used in sauces like the popular *molho de pimenta y limon* (pepper and lemon sauce) that accompanies roasts and traditional dishes. Indeed it ranks alongside salt and pepper as a catchall seasoning.

Brazilians must number as the most enthusiastic coffee-drinkers in the world. It is not unusual to consume anywhere from 12 to 24 *demitasses* – the tiny cups in which shots of coffee are served a day, at regular intervals and after all meals. In fact, all government agencies and private companies make it a point to serve coffee at least twice a day – making it the most widely practised daily ritual in Brazil.

feijoada

1 Pick over beans, wash and soak overnight in cold water. 2 Soak jerked beef, tongue, Canadian bacon overnight in separate pans of cold water. 3 On the day of cooking, drain the beans, cover with fresh cold water, and then cook for about 2½ hours in a covered saucepan. Add water, if needed, to keep the beans covered. When beans are cooked, remove ¼ cup of liquid and set aside to cooled. 4 While the beans are cooking, remove the meat from the liquids. 5 Drain the jerked beef, cover with additional cold water, boil and simmer for 1 hour or till fork tender. Remove and cut into 2.5-cm strips, set aside. 6 Parboil tongue till the skin is able to be removed, set aside. 7 Prick fresh sausages, parboil, then set aside. 8 Parboil Canadian bacon, spare ribs, smoked sausages and pig's feet, set aside. 9 Place all meats, except the fresh sausages but including the beef and bacon, in a very large saucepan. Cover with tepid water, and then bring to a boil. Simmer until the meats are tender, about 1½ hours. 10 Drain all the meats and add to the beans with the pork sausages, then simmer till meats are tender. Season with salt. 11 ½ hour before serving, sauté garlic and onions with shortening in a large skillet. Add optional ingredients at this time. 12 Add about 2 cups of the bean liquid over the mixture, simmer until mixture thickens, then return to the pot containing the beans and meats, simmer about ½ hours till thoroughly blended. Season to taste.

Recipe courtesy of Brazilian Cookery, Traditional and Modern by Margarette De Andrade.

5 cups black beans
500 g jerked beef
1 small smoked tongue
250 g Canadian bacon
500 g fresh pork sausages
500 g corned spareribs
500 g smoked sausages
  or Portuguese sausages
2 pig's feet
500 g lean beef,
  cut in two pieces
125 g lean bacon
1 tbsp shortening
2 large onions, chopped
3 garlic cloves, crushed

optional
1 tomato, chopped
1 tbsp parsley, chopped
1 hot pepper, crushed

chile

Chilean cuisine ranks as one of the most distinctive of South America. It is partly inspired by the long thin shape of their country, whose diverse neighbours range from the Atacama Desert (north), to the Andes (east), to the frozen Antarctic (south) and the southern Pacific Ocean (west). The ocean provides Chile with abundant fish and shellfish, which is why seafood takes centre stage in Chilean cuisine.

Desayuno (continental breakfast) typically starts a Chilean day, a simple coffee or tea with milk and toast. Later in the day, typical Chilean dishes eaten at lunch include *escabeche* (pickled hen or quail aspic), *carne mechada* (roast beef flavoured with vegetables and *guiso de repollo morado* or *chocute* (red cabbage and apple stew), accompanied by Chilean wines. No Chilean repast is complete without the *chupe de mariscos* (shellfish, bread and cheese casserole), usually considered a test of the consummate chef. For *postres* (desserts), try the *maicena con leche* (cornstarch pudding) or *papayas en almibar* (papayas in syrup), served with *mistela* (a fruit-based after-dinner liqueur), brandy or *aguitas calientes* (hot herbal teas) as an after-meal beverage.

Afternoon tea, or *onces*, often comprises hot tea, *mate* or *chuno* with some sweet bread, cookies, cake or small sandwiches. This should last till *cena* (dinner or supper), usually consisting of soup or vegetable casserole and a dessert. Chilean cuisine is a harmonious blend of Old World Spanish and New World cuisines (*cocina criolla Chilena*). Their food is wonderfully varied, richly flavoured and always enjoyable.

2 kg medium potatoes,
  cooked and mashed
250 g butter, melted
2 cups warm milk
¼ cup cream
4 eggs, hard-boiled and sliced
250 g black olives
2 egg whites,
  beaten with 1 tbsp sugar

filling
1 kg ground beef
2 onions, finely chopped
1 tbsp *paprika*
2 tbsp oil
½ bell pepper, finely chopped
250 g raisins
1 tbsp oregano
½ tbsp cumin
½ tbsp pepper
1 tbsp parsley, finely chopped
1 red pepper, finely chopped
salt to taste

pastel de papas (potato casserole)

1 Add the milk, cream and butter to the mashed potatoes, blend well. This mixture must be soft and not too dry. Whip until smooth and season to taste.
2 Fry the onion and *paprika* in the oil. Add the meat and the rest of the filling ingredients. Season to taste and continue to cook over low heat until done.
3 In an oven-proof casserole dish, place the filling on the bottom, cover with slices of eggs and olives. Cover with the mashed potato mixture. Baste with the beaten egg whites. 4 Place in an oven on moderate heat to brown and serve immediately. 5 Serves 10.

south america

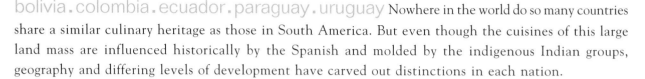

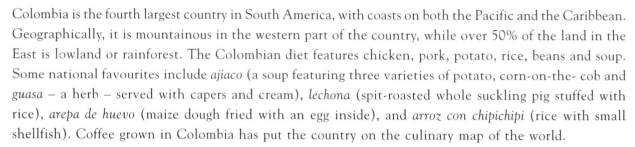

bolivia. colombia. ecuador. paraguay. uruguay Nowhere in the world do so many countries share a similar culinary heritage as those in South America. But even though the cuisines of this large land mass are influenced historically by the Spanish and molded by the indigenous Indian groups, geography and differing levels of development have carved out distinctions in each nation.

Colombia is the fourth largest country in South America, with coasts on both the Pacific and the Caribbean. Geographically, it is mountainous in the western part of the country, while over 50% of the land in the East is lowland or rainforest. The Colombian diet features chicken, pork, potato, rice, beans and soup. Some national favourites include *ajiaco* (a soup featuring three varieties of potato, corn-on-the- cob and *guasa* – a herb – served with capers and cream), *lechona* (spit-roasted whole suckling pig stuffed with rice), *arepa de huevo* (maize dough fried with an egg inside), and *arroz con chipichipi* (rice with small shellfish). Coffee grown in Colombia has put the country on the culinary map of the world.

Ecuadorian food comprises mainly soups and stews, corn pancakes, rice, potato, eggs, vegetables, bananas and excellent seafood. Dishes like *caldo de pates* (a soup made from cattle hooves), *cuy* (whole roasted guinea pig), *corvina* (sea bass) served *frito* (fried), *apanada* (breaded and fried) and a *la plancha* (filleted) are typical offerings, often served with *salsa picant* (a spicy dipping sauce made from chili peppers) on the side. The ubiquitous *chucula* (made from boiled plantains) is a popular beverage. Bolivia is South America's fifth largest country and is roughly the size of France and Spain combined. Some signature dishes of Bolivia are *salteñas* (oval-shaped pastry stuffed with heavily-spiced meat and vegetable), *papas rellenas* (stuffed potatoes), *escabeche* (carrots, onions and peppers pickled in vinegar), *chupe* (a thick meat, vegetable and grain soup flavoured with garlic, tomato, cumin and hot pepper). *Ckocko* (spicy chicken cooked in wine or *chicha* and served with *choclo*, olives, grated orange peel and other aromatic condiments) and *fritanga* (spicy hot pork with mint and *maize hominy*) are two other examples of the diversity and versatility of Bolivian cuisine. The people in Paraguay and Uruguay are predisposed to a diet of meat. Corn and yucca, and their derivatives, usually accompany each meal. Favourite dishes include *mbaiby so-ó* (hot maize pudding with chunks of meat), *sooyo sopy* (a thick soup made with ground meat and served with rice or noodles) in Paraguay, and *parrillada* (beef platter), *chivito* (steak sandwich with all the trimmings) and *húngaros* (spicy sausage in a hot-dog roll) in Uruguay.

pernil de cerdo (herb-roasted leg of pork)

1 Grind onion and all the herbs together, then use it to marinate the leg of pork. Let stand overnight. At two hour intervals, sprinkle salt over the leg of pork. This will give it a crispy texture when roasted. **2** Set the oven to about 170 degrees Celsius. Roast the leg of pork for about two hours. For medium done roast, reduce heat to 130 degrees Celsius and continue to bake for another hour maximum. For well done, leave it at 170 degrees Celsius for the remaining hour. **3** Baste the leg with olive oil and sweet white wine at intervals. **4** About 10 minutes from removing the leg from the oven, glaze the meat with honey to give it a golden brown look.

2 kg leg of pork,
  with the skin on
2 large white onions
1 red capsicum
2 cups sweet white wine
1 tbsp cinnamon
5½ clovers *Mayoran*
4½ bay leaves
½ tsp thyme
olive oil
honey

peru

From the Andean highlands of Cuzco (home of the ancient Inca stronghold of Macchu Picchu) to the coastal regions of Lima, the food of Peru is as varied as the country's diverse geography. Fresh seafood from the country's position right on the Humboldt Current (a stream of cold water producing a wealthy array of fish) is a national delicacy. And the fertile valleys between the tropical jungles of the Amazon and the frigid plateaus of the Andes provide the backdrop of a food culture that is as old as civilisation itself.

Thousands of years ago, the Incas deified the potato and peanut. No celebration existed without their consumption. Gold ingots (Peru is one of the world's leading gold producers) were made in the shape of potatoes, while peanuts were steeped in alcohol to produce *chicha de mani*, a drink drunk at any festivity. Other homegrown produce that have earned international renown are the nutritious, high-protein cereals, *quinoa* and *kiwwicha*, both of which are featured in the diets of space-bound NASA astronauts.

No discussion of Peruvian cuisine is complete without the mention of *pisco*. This grape brandy is borne from the fertile desert land and is the result of both Indian and Spanish cultures. *Pisco* means 'little bird' and the unique grapes from which the drink is made are grown mainly around the city of the same name. At 42 % proof, this firewater is likely to leave first time drinkers with more than a memory.

In 1848, a great wave of Chinese immigrants arrived in Peru searching for gold. As expected from the Chinese, they brought with them a strong culture of food. Soya sauce, rice and Oriental cooking techniques like stir-frying were introduced to Peru for the first time. In over a century and a half, the Chinese influence on Peruvian cuisine has been so significant that no Peruvian meal is now complete without the presence of rice. The impact is found in language itself as Peruvians now call ginger *kion*, and soya sauce *sillau* – the Cantonese names in both cases. In Lima alone, there are upwards of 1,500 Chinese restaurants.

Peru is unlike any other country in Latin America. Its blend of Spanish, African and Asian heritage has produced a culture and cuisine that is a melting pot of its inhabitants. Indeed, Peruvian cuisine is the epitome of fusion food before the latter became fashionable.

ceviche de pescado

If there is one representative dish of Peru, it is *ceviche*. Thousands of years before the Spanish arrived in Peru, coastal dwellers dined on raw seafood seasoned with *aji* chili pepper and other local spices. The Spanish, however, brought the first green lemons, the juice of which created a dynasty of raw dishes in the land.

1 Cut the fish in small chunks and put them in a big serving dish. **2** Season with salt, garlic, and chili. **3** Add the lemon juice and let settle. **4** Add the onion, chopped in small rings. **5** Serve with lettuce, camote, potatoes and corn. Add extra ground chili if desired.

1 kg fish fillet
2 cloves garlic, crushed
4 yellow fresh chilies, ground
2 *rocotos*
10 lemons, juice only
150 gm onions
lettuce, camotes, corn, potatoes as accompaniment
salt and pepper to taste

south america

guyana . suriname . venezuela Guyana is about the size of the United Kingdom, and is flanked by Venezuela on the West, Suriname on the East and Brazil on the South. The influences of the Creoles along with those of India, Africa, China, England, Portugal and North America have given Guyanese food its distinctive flavour. Typical Guyanese food found its roots in Creole dishes with an emphasis on seafood. The national favourite is a traditional Christmas dish, the pepper pot – essentially a spicy meat stew cooked in the bitter cassava juice, peppers and herbs. A meal is often built around a staple of rice accompanied by abundant seafood, tropical fruit and vegetables.

Suriname lies on the northern coast of South America and is an unusual cultural enclave with an extraordinary ethnic variety. Her multi-cultural disposition is the result of Dutch colonisation, the arrival of African slaves and foreign workers from India and Indonesia. As the result of these, Suriname's food is an exotic mix of East Indian, Indian, Creole and Chinese cuisines. The favourite dishes here include *rijstafel* (a variety of Dutch-inspired rice and dishes), *nasi goreng* (fried rice), *bakmi goreng* (fried noodles with beef and soya beancurd) and other spicy dishes of meat and vegetables.

The cuisine of Venezuela may be best described as eccentric and eclectic as it is a combination of sophistication and simplicity. The national fast food and staff of life is *arepa*, a flattened fist-sized ball of fried corn or wheat flour, widely consumed by rich and poor alike. When it is served in restaurants, *arepa* is eaten with *natilla*, a light cream cheese. The all-time favourite dish is *pabellón criollo*, a mound of shredded beef spiced with onion, green pepper, tomato, coriander and garlic, eaten with white rice, black beans and fried plantains, and accompanied by the ubiquitous *arepa*.

Other signature dishes of Venezuela include *tequeño* (an egg pastry dough wrapped around strips of cheese and rolled into cigar-sized or cucumber-sized rods, then fried); *hallaca* (cornmeal dough wrapped around chicken, pork and beef that is spiced with green pepper, onion, garlic, parsley, pork fat, olive oil, then wrapped and steamed in banana leaves); *sancocho* (a chunky stew); *consome de chipi chipi* (a thin broth with tiny clams); and *churros* (crispy fried pastry tubes sprinkled with sugar and served with hot chocolate). Their unique dessert, *bienmesabe*, is a dreamy sponge cake doused in coconut cream. Usually accompanied by coffee, it forms an integral part of the Venezuelan lifestyle.

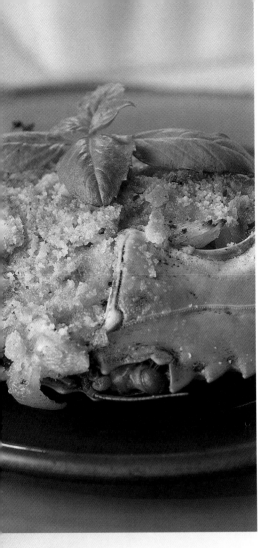

crab backs

1 Obtain live crabs at least one day before they are required and feed them with wholesome food, e.g. bread, peppers, leaves, etc. 2 Place the crabs in a large pan and pour in enough boiling water to cover. Discard this water. Wash the crabs and boil them for half an hour to loosen the flesh. 3 Remove the claws, cut open and pick out the meat. Remove the body from the shell, carefully preserving any eggs or fat, and discarding the gall which clings to the shell. Scrub the shells thoroughly and set aside. 4 Brown onions and shallots in the butter. Add the crab meat, piquante sauce, salt and pepper. 5 Refill the shells with the crab meat, then sprinkle with dried bread crumbs and a small dab of butter. 6 Brown in a quick oven. Garnish with *wirri-wirri* pepper and parsley before serving.

1 dozen crabs
2 – 3 tbsp butter or
    margarine
1 onion, chopped
2 – 3 shallots, chopped
1 tbsp piquante sauce,
    or *Worcestershire* sauce
salt and pepper
dried bread crumbs

garnish
wiri-wiri pepper (small
    berry-like hot red peppers,
    with a very strong and
    characteristic flavour)
parsley

talcari de chivo (goat in wine sauce)

1 Wash the goat with the juice from the lemons. Cut into pieces and season with salt, pepper and garlic. Marinate overnight. 2 Sauté the goat with the olive oil, add the water and cook for 30 minutes over low heat. 3 Add the tomatoes, onions and *jalapeno* and mix well. Cook for another 30 minutes or till the meat is tender. 4 Add the wine and cook for another 20 minutes. 5 Season to taste and serve with rice.

1 kg goat or mutton
2 lemons
6 tomatoes, chopped
100 g *jalapeno* peppers
salt and black pepper
    to taste
1 cup water
4 cups red wine
200 g garlic, chopped
1 kg onions,
    chopped coarsely
⅛ cup olive oil

the world on a plate

Masterfully designed to appeal to the most discriminating consumer, *Corelle* dinnerware marries beauty and elegance with lasting durability. The brilliant white body and contemporary styling enhance food presentation, whilst the wide selection of shapes and patterns such as the latest elegant '*Plum*' collection fits every decor and occasion.

Created from a unique laminated glass material, *Corelle* dinnerware has the appearance of fine china, with a distinct advantage – its thin, lightweight and stackable quality surpasses china. *Corelle* uses an exclusive process to bond the decoration and tableware into one timeless piece. This process guarantees uniform good looks that last, and is backed by a one year warranty against chipping, crazing and cracking.

The year 2000 marks a new corporate name and identity change for World Kitchen, Inc., formerly known as the Corning Consumer Products Company. World Kitchen looks forward to a new entrepreneurial spirit and global focus under its new corporate signature with well-known brands including *Corelle, Corningware, Visions, Pyrex, Revere, Baker's Secret, Chicago Cutlery, Regent Sheffield, OXO, EKCO and Grilla Gear.*

As a special accompaniment to *An Assembly of Taste – The Culinary World of the United Nations*, a limited edition plate is created for World Kitchen, Inc. by Immortal Design. Only 5000 *Corelle* plates, each featuring a delightful illustration of master chefs, have been produced to commemorate this publication of food notes and recipes from the 189 countries of the United Nations General Assembly.

This collector's item will go hand in hand with the anthology to acknowledge the significance of food in our global society. Together, they represent a celebration of life, and the colourful myriad of dishes that arrive at dining tables throughout the world.

WORLD KITCHEN

recipe index

AFRICAN ISLANDS

madagascar	lasopy, *vegetable soup*	79	entrée
	varenga, *roast shredded beef*	78	main dish
seychelles	ladob, *bananas and sweet potato in coconut milk*	79	dessert/snack
	shark chutney	79	main dish

MIDDLE EAST

israel	chicken braised in cider	84	main dish
lebanon	khobzi arabi, *middle-east flatbread*	83	entrée
	kibbi samak, *fish kibbe*	89	main dish
saudi arabia	najdi meat kabsah, *lamb stew with onion mixture*	86	main dish
united arab emirates	maj bus, *meat rice*	86	main dish

EASTERN EUROPE

czech republic	peceny kapr s kyselou omackou, *carp with sour cream sauce*	93	main dish
hungary	pork chops tokay style	100	main dish
poland	zur, *leavened meat and vegetable soup*	102	entrée
russian federation	blini, *russian crepes with sour cream*	95	entrée
	pashka, *russian easter dessert*	97	dessert/snacks
slovakia	houskove knedliky, *bun-dumpling*	93	entrée
	zemiakove sulane s makom, *potato noodles with poppy seeds*	93	entrée
ukraine	borscn, *beet soup*	96	entrée
	chicken kiev	97	main dish

BALKANS

croatia	janjetina ispod cripnje, *lamb baked under a cripnje*	99	main dish
	pisana pecenica 'stubica', *pork tenderloin stubica style*	99	main dish
macedonia	gravche-travce, *pan-fried beans*	99	entrée

SOUTH EASTERN EUROPE

armenia	lentil and bulgur cakes	104	entrée
	armenian pumpkin stew	105	main dish
turkey	hunkar begendi, *sultan's delight with eggplant purée*	107	main dish

CARIBBEAN

antigua and barbuda	salt fish and antrobers	154	main dish
	salted cod fish and eggplant		
	antigua doucouna,	155	main dish
	sweet potato dumplings		
	fungee	155	main dish
bahamas	johnny cakes	157	dessert/snack
	peas and rice	157	entrée
cuba	shrimp in creamy coriander sauce	157	main dish
jamaica	ackee and saltfish	159	main dish

SOUTH AMERICA

argentina	beef empanadas, *beef patties*	162	dessert/snack
brazil	feijoada, *meat and bean stew*	164	main dish
chile	pastel de papas, *potato casserole*	165	entrée
colombia	pernil de cerdo, *herb-roasted leg of pork*	166	main dish
guyana	crab backs	169	main dish
peru	ceviche de pescado, *marinated raw fish*	167	entrée
venezuela	talcari de chivo, *goat in wine sauce*	169	main dish